ITALIAN COUNTRY LIVING

Caroline Clifton-Mogg

photography by **Chris Tubbs**

RYLAND
PETERS
& SMALL

LONDON NEW YORK

SENIOR DESIGNER Sally Powell

SENIOR EDITOR Henrietta Heald

LOCATION RESEARCH Gabriella Le Grazie

PICTURE RESEARCH Emily Westlake

PRODUCTION MANAGER Patricia Harrington

ART DIRECTOR Gabriella Le Grazie

PUBLISHING DIRECTOR Alison Starling

First published in the United Kingdom in 2005
This paperback edition published in 2008
by Ryland Peters & Small
20–21 Jockey's Fields
London WC1R 4BW
www.rylandpeters.com

10 9 8 7 6 5 4 3 2

Text copyright © Caroline Clifton-Mogg 2005
Design and photographs copyright
© Ryland Peters & Small 2005

ISBN 978-1-84597-619-4

A CIP record for this book is available from the
British Library.

Printed and bound in China.

introduction

Italian ideas on decorative matters have influenced other European countries and cultures for more than 500 years. From the early Renaissance, it was Italian designs and styles that spread throughout Europe, and Italian artists and craftsmen who put those new ideas into practice.

Not much has changed. In modern furniture design, for example, it is still Italian designers who introduce the new, the innovative, the exciting; who suggest the new materials and new methods of production that keep modern interior design alive.

Yet, paradoxically, Italy is also a country of history, a place where the past is always present. Indeed, it is somewhere where the past sometimes seems more important than the present. This is a feeling often demonstrated in the way that Italian country houses are decorated – particularly in the Tuscan countryside, where many of the houses in this book can be found.

This layering of past and present manifests itself as a style that borrows and adapts from other eras and places, editing and refining as it goes, and culminating in a look that is stylish, original and always comfortable and easy to live with. Unlike other European countries

such as France and, in particular, England, there was never in Italy a traditional country-house style, since the middle classes tended to settle in the towns and cities. The countryside belonged to the farmers and their workers, who furnished their homes relatively simply, without the touches of middle-class comfort and decoration that were so often employed elsewhere.

The postwar flight to the towns in Italy left many farmhouses of all sizes and descriptions to crumble into near-ruinous states. That, coupled with – particularly in some parts of Tuscany – extremely strict planning laws and vetoes on the building of new structures, has meant that, for most recent buyers, restoration and embellishment of an existing structure has been the only option – transforming stables and barns into habitable areas, rationalizing farm workers' quarters into comfortable and individual living space.

This relative creative freedom within the confines of a prescribed space has resulted in an individuality and inventiveness not often seen elsewhere; although the houses featured here are all different, and cannot easily be categorized or pigeonholed, they all share one important thing: an innate style and confidence that is utterly and completely Italian.

the elements

colour and texture

The colours and textures used in an interior – whether it's a rambling country farmhouse or a small studio – are the first things that one sees and feels on entering. Their importance in the overall design is paramount and they set the tone for the rest of the decorative scheme.

The colour and textures that go to make up the basic framework of Italian country style are as much to do with the landscape as with any carefully thought-out man-made scheme. Historically, the Italians have always been close – very close –'to the land and, since many of their country houses today are converted and reclaimed farmhouses and barns, it is fitting that this should be the case.

Traditionally, the group of colours used decoratively in the houses of the Italian countryside – both inside and out – were the colours of the land and the earth. Since the earliest times, man has used the naturally occurring pigments of the earth around him to extract colour; by the Middle Ages he had begun to refine – frequently by heating – the more basic earth tones into richer, deeper variants. These pigments were, and often still are, used to make distemper-like washes to be used both inside and out. Warm reds, ochres, umbers – every shade from reddish pink to golden brown – dress the walls and floors in an Italian interior. The depth of colour is sometimes achieved

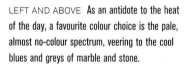

LEFT AND ABOVE As an antidote to the heat of the day, a favourite colour choice is the pale, almost no-colour spectrum, veering to the cool blues and greys of marble and stone.

BELOW LEFT The soft blue-grey of the walls and the traditionally designed metal bed make a cool haven from the summer sun.

OPPOSITE, ABOVE LEFT AND CENTRE These warm, earth-based tones are often pure pigment, mixed straight into the plaster as it is applied. It is the naturalness of these colours that makes them so admired – that and the way they bring summer into the house.

OPPOSITE, ABOVE RIGHT Graded tones from orange to yellow are used the length of a corridor wall; a dark green, painted stripe makes a trompe l'oeil skirting. A gauzy yellow and orange curtain accentuates the colours.

OPPOSITE, BELOW LEFT In an upstairs corridor, the walls and woodwork are painted in dark stripes of ochre, terracotta, pink and white. Instead of contrasting with these deep colours, the door curtains are designed to match.

OPPOSITE, BELOW RIGHT The strong ochre tone used on the walls of this living room holds its own against the bright Tuscan sun, and there is no contrast of colour: both furnishings and floor complement the wall tone.

with painted plaster and sometimes by adding the pigment to the wet plaster. Brighter colours are also found, but these will always be tempered by the earth – blues will usually have a touch of brown, reds and yellows a rich warmth.

Another palette favoured – particularly by those who undertake the restoration of old, sometimes dark buildings – is the 'no-colour' palette. Faced with a hot climate much of the year, dramatic scenery and the resultant glaring contrasts of light and shade, both inside and outside the house, many people use neutral tones – from pale grey to cream, stone and milky white – to offset textiles and furnishings in the house, as well as the movement and colour of country life.

Italian country life is to a large extent an outdoor life and this is reflected inside as well as out. The earth colours are offset by natural textures that come so easily to hand, from cane and wood, terracotta and iron to hand-painted faïence dishes and earthenware pots and bowls. It is rare to enter a house in the Italian countryside that does not have some or all of these materials on display and in daily use. Modern materials are not so often seen, although concrete, polished and coloured, is increasingly used on the floor.

LEFT A full-length corner cupboard has been painted and decorated in a semi-architectural style; the colour works perfectly with the ochre wall as well as with the grey-painted wooden daybed upholstered in complementary fabrics.

RIGHT A deep buttoned crimson cushion brightens up this dark wooden daybed.

OPPOSITE, ABOVE LEFT A white-painted classical console table is placed against a strong yellow wall and emphasized by the unusual pleated lampshade, the two mounted horns and a set of ornamental animal prints.

OPPOSITE, ABOVE RIGHT Ethnic-inspired textiles are popular in Italian country houses and are often used as furnishings and curtains.

furniture and fabrics

Traditionally, country furniture was of the type known as 'brown furniture', usually handed down through generations. Although some old pieces were heavy and cumbersome and are now out of favour, others, particularly those designed for practicality, are just as much admired and used today as ever they were.

In the kitchen, customarily the heart of the rural home – as well as, often, the warmest place in the building – the central table was all-important. Sturdy in construction and large enough to seat a number of people, it was used both to prepare food and to eat at, both inside the house and, in summer, brought outside under the trees.

Most households also had at least one large wooden cupboard – used in the kitchen for utensils, crockery and dried food, but also elsewhere in the house, to store clothing and bed linen; these solid cupboards were usually unadorned, but sometimes might be painted and decorated in bright and vibrant tones. Iron is another traditional material – the ironworker was once a familiar sight in Italian towns – and, in company with wood, it was the most popular material for beds. Many of these decorative beds are still seen today, sometimes painted, sometimes polished and always original.

Although these antiques can still be found in abundance, in many modern Italian country houses, items of old country furniture are

BELOW This iron bed with its domed canopy was made in Tuscany but based on a French campaign bed. It is an excellent example of the ironworker's art and, as such, is too pretty and intriguing to drape with curtains. Simple white linen and a traditional quilt suffice.

RIGHT A clever decorative scheme involves five different textile designs – all used in close proximity to each other and yet with no sense of excess; the secret is that they are all in the same colour combination of red and white, and four of them are based on geometric patterns.

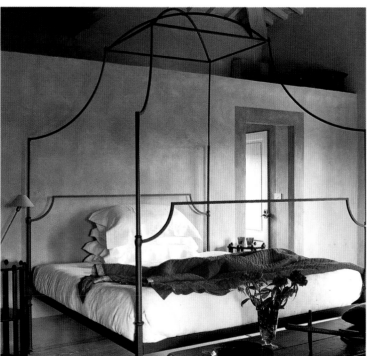

RIGHT A pair of cupboard doors and the bedroom door between them have been painted in a design that unites and unifies all three.

FAR RIGHT Two old-fashioned chairs have been upholstered so as to emphasize their design while wittily exaggerating their style.

BELOW The essential storage cabinets in this kitchen are cleverly set into the walls behind pairs of old shutters.

BELOW RIGHT All the furniture pieces in this bedroom, both wooden and iron, are traditional Tuscan; seen against a plain white background, their charm can be appreciated in a new way.

LEFT A much admired facet of Italian country style is the combination of what one might call retro-chic with classical taste. This arrangement is a bright example: the circular table has been covered with a traditional cloth, and a collection of Capo di Monte ceramics and offbeat floral displays is lit by a contemporary lamp designed by Roberto Gerosa.

BELOW The simplicity of painted blue and white stripes on the wall, combined with natural white bed hangings and plain linen curtains, means that the bed itself can carry a much bolder blue and white toile de Jouy quilted cover, as well as a couple of exuberant printed cotton cushions in the same style.

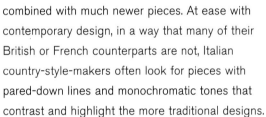

combined with much newer pieces. At ease with contemporary design, in a way that many of their British or French counterparts are not, Italian country-style-makers often look for pieces with pared-down lines and monochromatic tones that contrast and highlight the more traditional designs.

Much the same approach can be seen in the Italian attitude towards fabrics. Although from the 14th to the 17th centuries the Italians were renowned throughout Europe for the richness and splendour of their woven silk velvets and brocades, today's tastes – or country tastes, at any rate – are generally less elaborate.

Antique textiles are still on the whole much prized, and often used folded on a bed or draped over a chair, but are used less frequently than new, natural fabrics. The vogue is for pale, bleached or softly coloured linens, stripes of every description, and ethnic, especially oriental and African, designs, which seem to have a particular affinity with the Italian landscape and light.

outdoor living

Life outdoors no longer frightens us. Even in the greyest of climes, summer sees a rush to set up tables and chairs outside, however small the patch or dark the day. For all that, it is the Italians who do it best – for they have long understood the charms and pleasures that come from living outside.

For an Italian who spends time in the countryside, outdoor living is as much a part of the experience as life indoors. There is no barrier and no distinction between spaces; from the earliest part of the day to the often balmy evenings, Italians eat, sleep, work and relax outside.

In Italy there has always been an affinity with the land surrounding a house, and Italian gardens, half architecture and half horticulture, have been famous, and influential, since the time of the first Roman emperors. Study the remains of Hadrian's garden outside Rome – a verdant pleasure dome designed as a series of outdoor rooms and studded with architectural features, pools and dramatic columns of stone and marble. In complete contrast, 1,400 years later, at the villas

TOP, LEFT TO RIGHT A terrace on which to dine is a vital part of rural life. Simple pots of scented geraniums look as pretty and natural as their surroundings. The swimming pool and paved area have been laid out so as not to detract from the striking woodland landscape.

BOTTOM, LEFT TO RIGHT The same stone has been used for the terrace and the house's exterior walls. This stark poolscape has been designed to stand up to its dramatic setting. A wooden pergola lightly shading a dining area is every summer-lover's dream.

designed by Andrea Palladio in the 16th century, the land came right up to the house, with little attempt at designing a formal garden that would come between the living quarters and the landscape.

In modern Italian country life, the basic outside necessities are few – sometimes a pool, but always a flat space of ground close to the house that is usually designed as a simple terrace, left in its natural state or laid with stone, local brick or hard-wearing terracotta tiles.

A pergola is another essential. It may be wood or metal, traditional or modern, but, whatever the details of the structure, it is always large enough to shelter a table and chairs for leisurely dining. Another form of shelter, and a very Italian one, is the loggia – a shady, roofed structure, attached to the house or set apart, where eating, sleeping and reading can all be pursued in shady seclusion.

THIS PAGE AND OPPOSITE Quite as much care is taken with the spaces outside the house as with those within, and the shady, peaceful courtyards and gardens of Italian country houses are places in which to linger. Stone masonry is an important part of the Italian building tradition, and stone – often decoratively combined with brick – is extensively used throughout Italy to make walls and doorways, as well as terraces, paths and steps.

the homes

Rustic Italian style is neither old-fashioned nor naïve; it is a celebration of all that is natural, and is based on the traditions of the surrounding area. Admirers of the style favour an earthy colour palette and look for locally made furniture and objects that they can put to the use for which they were intended.

rustic

LEFT La Lite is a farmhouse that, like so many in the area, was constructed over a long period, and this is reflected in its almost organic appearance. Toia Saibene and the Magnificos were anxious that it should reflect its history as a working house on a large estate. The land has always been cultivated here, and olive trees are still grown there today.

an earthy simplicity

La Lite – the Tuscan home of Toia Saibene, her sister Giuliana and Giuliana's husband Federico Magnifico – is an old, partly restored farmhouse near Lucignano; they bought the house in 1979 from the Marchese Lotaringi della Stufa, who still lives in the nearby Castello del Calcione, which itself dates from 1483.

LEFT A house in the Italian countryside must have enough shade close to the house to make life pleasant during long sunny, summer days and it was a priority for Toia Saibene and her sister and brother-in-law to make a space, or spaces, where they could eat and live outside in summer. This sheltered spot, surrounded by mellow stone and brick walls, was perfect for the wooden pergola that they constructed along one wall as well as for the long table that they found in a local church; the whole scene epitomizes the charm of Italian outdoor life.

RIGHT The family were careful to furnish the house simply and with suitably rustic furniture. This corner of the living room is furnished not only with a local Tuscan desk but also a quirky, woven-seated childbirth chair also found locally.

Traditionally, La Lite had been inhabited by peasant families who cultivated the land for themselves and gave a share of the produce to the landlord in return. This was part of a system set up several hundred years previously – the earliest part of the house dates from the 17th century – and over the years the land had been used to grow olive trees, vines, wheat and mulberry trees for silkworms.

When Toia and her family first saw the house, it had been abandoned for 20 years and needed a great deal of work to make it habitable. Their intention was to return the house to its original look and character – that of a peasants' house on a working estate. There was also a large amount of reconstruction to be done outside: since the house had been neglected for such a long time, it was necessary to re-establish the plantation of olive trees and also to allow the land to recuperate. It

BELOW RIGHT The interior is planned as carefully as the exterior. A traditional kitchen sink has above it a Tuscan plate cabinet – not only an extremely practical piece of storage, but also a satisfying piece of rural design.

RIGHT Although these objects come from different parts of Italy – the white chunky china is from Puglia and the handmade basket was made locally in Tuscany – they are all rustic in concept and design.

Their intention was to return the house to its original look and character – that of a peasants' house on a working estate.

was not possible to restore the living plan entirely to its original layout, which had allowed for family life on the first floor while the ground floor held the stables and pigsty as well as storage for farm machinery, utensils and some produce. Much basic work needed to be done: they replaced the roof, installed a heating system and rewired the property. They also added two bathrooms.

La Lite now consists of a large kitchen, living room and five bedrooms. Throughout the house Toia and her family used the original materials as far as they could and, luckily, were able to keep the existing walls and floors and the original kitchen sink, as well as the large fireplace.

That the family have succeeded in their aims is abundantly clear: each room looks as though it has merely been rescued from some ancient sleeping spell – there is no suggestion of the type of major work that was undertaken. This illusion is helped by the choice of furnishings and decorative processes. 'With the furnishings, we have tried to maintain the original peasant style, choosing simple rustic furniture that we bought in the nearby village,' says

THIS PAGE The scene that greets guests in the dining area of La Lite's kitchen is dominated by a Tuscan wooden table and matching benches dating from the 19th century. The very early 18th-century black-glazed pot in the centre of the table is from Cortona, while the elongated metal chandelier was made in the 1930s in Lombardy.

LEFT Toia Saibene's bedroom is a symphony of the colours of the Tuscan countryside, from the terracotta floor tiles to the original red-brown shutters and the quilted bedcover. The bed, as so much else in the house, is Tuscan.

RIGHT On a table in Toia's bedroom is a small collection of salt-glazed pottery from Piedmont.

FAR RIGHT A country bench with its integral storage chest becomes the centrepiece of a satisfying rustic tableau – which incorporates everything around it, from the sabots on the floor to the hand-made baskets on the seat and the decorative straw hats on the wall.

BELOW An ultra-rustic-chic dormitory: three matching Tuscan peasant beds with imposing, raised headboards have been arranged beside matching Tuscan bedside tables; narrow-striped bedcovers add to the room's austere formality.

'We have tried to maintain the original peasant style, choosing simple rustic furniture that we bought in the nearby villages.'

Toia. The walls are plastered, using a finish known as *a calce*, where colour is added directly to the plaster, and the windows are painted in a brick colour as they would originally have been. The fabrics used are simple in design and found locally; the one exception is the room in which the family have used Indian fabrics bought on their travels.

Outside, the warm tones of the outer walls invite peace and quiet in the sun; these external walls are made in typical Tuscan style, which alternates stone and brick. They added a pergola, to provide the necessary shade in this often very hot part of the country, and a long table, which they found in a local church.

It is not as easy as it might appear to restore a house in the style in which it was originally designed while also making it functional. It is a testament to the trio that they have succeeded so well in capturing the best of traditional rural life while ensuring that beneath the timeless surface are all the essential underpinnings of modern life.

OPPOSITE Enclosed by roughly hewn stone walls, this haphazardly charming area of the house now serves as part conservatory and part entrance to the kitchen.

LEFT Outside the front door is a bread oven set into the wall; it is not the original oven, but, rather, a smaller version designed to replace it and built by Vanni Calamai.

BELOW From a narrow hallway a set of steps leads up to bedrooms; all the colours here, used in bold patches, and based on an earth palette, are carefully chosen to complement each other.

the tower house

The ancient tower that forms the centrepiece of this country home is a striking and formidable presence in the Chianti countryside. The tower was constructed in about 1200 as a defence post, with stables at ground level and living quarters above.

Nicoletta and Vanni Calamai are not the first to have lived here and nor, probably, will they be the last, but their tenure to date has lasted almost 30 years. In that time they have adapted and fashioned the original tower, which now houses the bedrooms, and the surrounding buildings that had been added over the centuries, into an individual and comfortable home, using wherever possible the original materials and structure of the rooms.

Before the Calamais moved in, the building had been occupied by farm workers before being abandoned for 20 years. The gradual restoration is continuing. 'I like moving things and decorating, and I like messing around with furniture and flowers,' says Nicoletta. The result does not, of course, look 'messed around'; it looks extremely cosy and as if it had always been the way it is today. This is deliberate, since neither Nicoletta nor Vanni like the idea of contemporary fittings in an ancient

ABOVE AND OPPOSITE The kitchen, carved out of the old stables, exudes an air of friendly, comfortable informality, with everything on hand for the preparation and cooking of food. Vanni Calamai, known for his handiwork in the house, made the wooden surround to the stone sink, which doubles as a handsome container.

ABOVE RIGHT Vine tomatoes are hung to dry from a metal device suspended from a shelf.

RIGHT The substantial kitchen fireplace has been set up as it might have been centuries ago, with a well-used cooking pot hanging from a trivet above the fire.

house. For example, the kitchen, which leads off a conservatory entrance, is studiously low-key, with fittings hidden from sight. Once the stables, it now has the appearance of a comfortable living room.

As Nicoletta explains, 'In these country houses, the kitchen is the first room you step into. So we didn't want it to be too kitchen-y in appearance; it had to be comfortable too. It's the room with the fireplace and where we have breakfast, lunch and dinner when we are not outside – and that's six months of the year. It is also the living room (with a television set hidden in the fireplace).' Many of the fittings – such as the slatted wooden chairs around

LEFT In the main bedroom an old English commode chair has been granted a new lease of life as a desk chair – a perfect partner for the late 19th-century wooden bureau.

BELOW When is a bathroom an unconventional bathroom – or even no bathroom at all? Answer: when it is designed as a comfortable corner in an otherwise traditionally furnished room.

All through the house are interesting objects collected on the owners' travels, and charmingly arranged with quirky mixtures and juxtapositions of colour and shape.

LEFT Under a set of stairs built by the farmers who once lived in the house, the Calamais have cleverly constructed a study area, where once there was a very basic kitchen. A painted dado line divides the wall into separate areas of colour, picked up by the tones of the paintings on the wall and easel by artist Christine Szabo.

OPPOSITE, BELOW RIGHT With its 200-year-old terracotta floor and its original vaulted ceiling, the main bedroom is a charming place, made more so by the traditional Tuscan iron bed married with an 18th-century Venetian mirror above the bedside table. The division of the wall and vaulted ceiling into two with a painted line is a device that draws attention to the curves and angles of the ceiling.

the table, the wooden worktop with its inset sink – were made by Vanni Calamai, a self-confessed DIY enthusiast who likes nothing better than to work with wood, old and new. 'He adores fixing old objects and making them work,' says Nicoletta.

The bathroom creates a similar impression to the kitchen. It feels like a comfortable room that happens to be, by chance, somewhere you can have a bath. As Nicoletta explains, 'In the old country houses there was no bathroom – just a "hanging" that resembled a loo. So, at a certain moment, people chose a room, usually a big room, and transformed it into a bathroom. This meant that there was plenty of space, so plenty of things ended up there.' Nicoletta's talent is for decorating and arranging the furniture and objects in the house,

many of which they have collected on their travels; all through the house are interesting objects, charmingly arranged with quirky combinations and juxtapositions of colour and shape.

She has a talent for arranging the space outside as well, dividing the area surrounding the tower into comfortable and relaxing areas from which to view the ever-changing landscape or simply to sit and relax. Many of these areas are furnished with tables made by Vanni, using the bases of local wine barrels.

La Torre del Chito is a truly relaxed and hospitable home. 'Though sometimes I think wistfully of a modern, well-equipped flat where everything works,' says Nicoletta, 'we love our old house, the space, the views and its warmth, even in winter. We are very happy here.'

LEFT Original beams, stone steps and a rediscovered archway are among the structural elements that define the ground floor of this restored farmhouse.

RIGHT The stone terrace outside the house gives far-ranging views of the surrounding countryside.

On the other side of the house, and invisible from inside, is a swimming pool looking over yet another spectacular landscape.

ABOVE The owners wanted to furnish the house simply and sympathetically; they designed the console table in the hall.

among the olives

The British owners of this once abandoned farmhouse have achieved that for which so many inhabitants of cooler climes yearn. They have discovered a house in a beautiful part of the Italian countryside, restored it, and now live in it for much of the year.

It was not as easy as it sounds. First there was the finding, then there was the doing. 'We had been renting a property in the Chianti Classico area, dreaming of finding our own house,' explains one of the owners. 'We wanted to live close to a particular medieval abbey. In 1985 we found a farmhouse that had once belonged to the abbey, overlooking it and built on the end of a ridge, giving panoramas over three sides.' Unlike many other houses in the area, it was uninhabited but not entirely derelict.

As is the case with all abandoned farmhouses, there was an immense amount of work to be done to make it habitable. For example, the ground floor was made up of the original cowsheds. There was

THIS PAGE **Like every other room in the house, the kitchen is furnished and decorated in almost minimalist style. The wooden table is, unusually, graced with a marble top and the imposing kitchen fireplace was made, in part, with old door posts, found elsewhere.**

LEFT There is a simple stillness about this room, which gives it an instant appeal. It might emanate from the old kitchen table – the first piece of furniture brought to the house – or the traditional wooden chairs with their rush seats, or even from the old doors that hide from view the essentials of modern kitchen life.

BELOW LEFT This is a house where the basic structure matters. Leading up into the kitchen, this arch, with its attractive brickwork, was found and restored during the time of the initial construction work. Carefully chosen handmade terracotta tiles have been laid throughout, replacing the original dirt and rubble floor.

no functioning water supply or plumbing, and all the outbuildings were in a parlous state. The massive job of restoration began. Within two years the house was habitable, and work continued for a further three years after that because it was important to the couple to get the structure of the house right – to let it to speak for itself.

The harmonious result is an appealing four-bedroomed main house with a small guest house in an outbuilding. Architectural and structural triumphs include an archway leading into the kitchen, which was uncovered and restored with old stone steps, and a kitchen fireplace constructed from old door posts. On the floors upstairs are the original brick tiles and downstairs, where once there was only dirt and rubble, hand-made terracotta tiles have been laid. The kitchen, with its new-old fireplace and solid table, is the very heart of the house, as it traditionally was in all farmhouses, and the bedrooms exude an air of simple comfort.

The owners started with little furniture other than the old kitchen table. Slowly, though, they began to buy other pieces – 'an eclectic mix', they call it, with a preponderance of local antiques such as the charming painted cupboard in the bedroom; they even made some pieces themselves, such as a simple console table in the entrance

hall. Their taste is essentially minimalist, and the house is extremely uncluttered: 'We would rather have a few well-chosen things than a large number of objects that fill up every nook and cranny.'

Colour, in its purely decorative sense, is almost incidental; lime whitewash has been used on almost all the walls, with the exception of a couple of bedrooms and bathroom, which are painted in tones of yellow ochre. The owners feel that the house's architectural structure – the tones created by the light and shadow cast by the floors, walls and ceilings – creates its own colour scheme, to which it is unnecessary to add.

Outside, invisible from the house – and from just about anywhere else – is the swimming pool, which is set into an olive grove and edged with local stone. All around the pool and the house is a carefully nurtured natural landscape that supports more than 600 olive trees – something that the owners feel strongly about: 'If you live in an olive-producing area, it is important to celebrate it by surrounding yourself with these perennially beautiful and evocative trees.'

ABOVE AND OPPOSITE The owners relish the detail and charm of this elaborately painted antique cupboard with its panels of flower sprays, which they discovered in the area. Their taste is essentially minimalist, however, so every piece such as the painted cupboard is balanced by something else extremely simple – in this case, the modern divan bed and night table. The floor is also left uncovered, with no carpet or rug to detract from its natural state.

LEFT One of the joys of an old house is small niches, alcoves and spaces that can be usefully employed for new purposes.

The owners sought to emphasize the architecture's reassuring solidity and wonderful variety, believing that you should 'feel' the building around you as you walk through it.

The Italians understand contemporary style better than anyone; whether urban or rural, they bring to the genre unique confidence and elan. A modern rural interior might consist only of all that is new, but it is just as likely to contain a mixture of old favourites and new finds, all edited and refined into a recognizable simplicity of style.

contemporary

LEFT The living area, furnished with distinctive 19th-century scholarback oriental chairs, is part of what was formerly the teachers' common room. Mimmi has kept the original terrazzo floor, which is now warmed by a new fireplace that she designed and installed.

ABOVE AND RIGHT The school corridor with its original floor has deliberately been left unadorned except for the Indonesian door at the end, flanked by locally made iron lanterns. What were once the classrooms are now the bedrooms and lead off to the left.

an old school story

Mimmi O'Connell's retreat in the Val d'Orcia is a former school in the village of San Casciano dei Bagni: 'I loved the space of La Scuola; I wanted it as soon as I saw it,' says the designer. 'I once had a farmhouse in the village but this is different.'

La Vecchia Scuola, as it is sometimes known in the village, translates as 'the former school' rather than 'the charmingly old school' and, on the outside at least, it is not particularly charming at all. Built in the 1960s and designed, like many buildings of the period, for function rather than form, it is municipal in style, box-like and totally devoid of the nostalgic aura that permeates other, older country dwellings.

All that is fine with Mimmi O'Connell. She has already done the Tuscan farmhouse thing and moved on, and, as a modern designer of verve and invention, the open spaces and spatial qualities of the building – in particular, its long corridor, in

LEFT Designed for both cooking and eating, the kitchen has a single storage shelf running around the whole working area, an industrial cooker and cupboard doors painted in shiny white gloss. Traditional English country chairs are paired with an 18th-century Swedish table.

BELOW A glass honey pot sits on the Peperino stone work surface.

BOTTOM Always a stickler for detail, Mimmi has had special plates made particularly to be used in La Scuola.

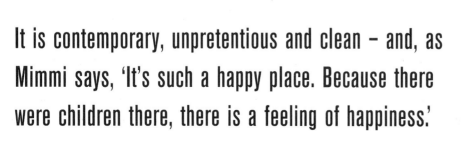

It is contemporary, unpretentious and clean – and, as Mimmi says, 'It's such a happy place. Because there were children there, there is a feeling of happiness.'

LEFT Behind the living area is the area for winter dining, where Mimmi O'Connell has once again successfully combined a number of different styles and periods. While the folding chairs came originally from a famous English public school, Winchester College, the new table, with its practical zinc top, is made by Conran, and the exotic candlesticks are from 16th-century Mongolia. Against the wall – throughout the house, all the pictures rest against the walls rather than being hung – is *Nuts and Bolts* by Ben Johnson, and a pile of English woven baskets is arranged in a corner in quasi-sculptural fashion. The windows are deliberately left uncurtained, and no rug mars the pristine terrazzo floor.

which you can still sense the sound of small, clattering feet – acted like a magnet on her acquisitive and decorative senses: 'The chance to make a house out of 560 square metres (6,000 square feet) of space, all on one floor, was one I couldn't miss – and a house with double-height ceilings, and fabulous views into the bargain.'

So Mimmi bought the school and set about getting the measure of the place. She wanted to make it into a comfortable house, while retaining the idea that it had been a working building. The school's architecture informed the design and decoration, which she felt should be disciplined and simple. So she cut new openings into the walls where hitherto there had been none, she replaced school

windows with French windows, and she built a fireplace inside. For the summer living area she built a portico and a pool area, reached from the house through four French windows and lined with local travertine, with woodwork painted grey; meals are taken here on large tables designed by Mimmi and made from scaffolding planks.

'I wanted to continue the sense of discipline that still hung in the air,' she says. The school corridor was a constant reminder of the building's original function, and Mimmi wanted it to dictate or at least influence the design and decoration. The floor of the corridor was the original, indestructible terrazzo – disliked by some for its industrial connotations, but liked by Mimmi for its association with the building's

LEFT The same sense of order that pervades the public areas of La Scuola is evident in bedrooms of almost monastical austerity, were it not for the luxurious bedding and linen. The six bedrooms in La Scuola are havens of peace and silence. The master bedroom (shown here) – like the other bedrooms, a former classroom – is dominated by a cast-iron, four-poster bed, which was designed by Mimmi after a French campaign bed and made in Tuscany by the craftsman who was responsible for many of the other iron pieces in the house.

BELOW In this double bedroom, both beds were designed by Mimmi and made in Tuscany. The painting, *The Visitor*, is by Sally Green.

OPPOSITE The beds are French, their swirling iron curves emphasized by the imaginative and unusual mirror, made from a mansard window.

former life. She has allowed the colour in the terrazzo to dictate the internal colour scheme – a mix of greys, terracotta, beige and a chalky white. Elsewhere, in each of the bedrooms (all former classrooms), she has used matt white on the walls, with glossy white on the deep skirting boards. She never hangs paintings; they are always left propped up against the walls.

This simple, unadorned interior makes a perfect background for her collection of Indonesian art – like the oversized pair of 18th-century horses and their riders, the antique, wooden wild boars, the old baskets and water containers. At the end of the otherwise unadorned corridor hangs an ornate and ornamental door from Lombok – a dramatic touch.

The severity of the design is touched throughout by softer details such as linen sheets and luxurious white towels, 19th-century Welsh blankets and bold Welsh quilts with intricate patterns – all of which come from her own shop, Port of Call in London. And there is comfort in the technology, too. In one room, a media wall is unapologetically dominated by a large plasma television.

It is difficult to tell from the sunny, light-filled interiors of Sebastian Abbado's Tuscan masterpiece that it was built in the 20th century – and as a machinery store at that. One large area on the ground floor combines a living space with a kitchen area that is dominated by a range, antique in appearance but modern in design. The textured concrete floor is covered with natural woven rugs and each object has a purpose that is practical as well as decorative. The relative sparseness is deliberate – he only wanted pieces of furniture and decorative accessories that could hold their own, and were interesting in their own right, and this he has achieved, using a clever mixture of the old and new, the western and the oriental; lighting is achieved with modern designs by Artemide.

an elegant artistry

Architect Sebastian Abbado's house in Tuscany is the proverbial bolt-hole. Once a barn used for the storage of farm machinery, it has been converted by him into a light and airy loft – a place which he can use as a base for his art and sculpture.

When Sebastian Abbado found his house, close to the home of his mother, Gabriella (see pages 88–93), it was a machinery store only in name; nothing remained except the perimeter and the foundations. But that was enough for him to work on. In common with many other places in Europe, in this part of Italy new building is permitted only within the original foundations of an existing building, and in the style of the original – which was, in this case, not much style at all, 'It was built in the mid 20th century and not very interesting,' says Sebastian. Not that he found this daunting – his architectural background meant that he looked at the project with interest rather than alarm.

'This is to be my private Tuscan den and it is, up to a point, a work-in-progress. It was meant to be a simple enclosure although it didn't turn out quite like that. It isn't finished yet – it's one of those places that constantly develops, but it will eventually become exactly what

RIGHT At one side of the living area is an all-purpose Tuscan table flanked by a church bench whose proportions make the two a fine match. An old metal hat stand is hung with empty picture frames as well as hats, and above the two doors leading from the room are framed tapestries that emphasize the architectural qualities of the mix. A painting by Althea Wilson is propped on the wooden French cupboard.

BELOW RIGHT Pride of place in this double bedroom is taken by the Italian iron bed dating from the early 19th century; green-painted wooden Italian chairs stand at the foot.

I want.' Sebastian was very clear in his own mind about what he wanted: 'I didn't want a townhouse or a very modern, minimalist place; it was to be light, and at the same time I wanted to keep the space itself sparse and furnished with essentials – pieces that each had their own space and were important enough to stand alone.'

This he has done: the simple pieces of furniture are well positioned, looking as he hoped – a little theatrical and sculptural at the same time. He dislikes rooms that are too full: 'If it's an object or even a blank wall, if it has something to say (and even a wall can speak), or if it has a purpose or a reason – then it can have a place here.'

Cleverly, each piece seems completely at home: 'I don't like it when an interior looks too researched or too obvious. Old houses that are completely modernized with new furniture seem to have lost their way, as do houses decorated the other way around – modern buildings with old things carefully placed within them never seem to work.'

The house today is perhaps larger than he originally envisaged. It has two double bedrooms with their own bathrooms, a single bedroom and a bed in an upper gallery; downstairs there is a large living area that incorporates a kitchen space, which

THIS PAGE Looking down the stairs into the ground-floor space from the gallery above, the precision of the placing of the furniture and objects can be appreciated. In the foreground is a distinctly Sebastian Abbado touch – a witty chandelier of red roses designed by Lorenzo Capaccio.

is fitted with an ingenious stove, similar in type to an Aga – a replica range that both heats the area and can be used for cooking.

The materials – such as the textured-concrete floors – are equally carefully thought out. Sebastian seeks to use natural materials where he can and chooses colours with a purpose: 'I like to use new varnishes, unusual pigments and colour to get a contrived ancient/modern look – again something that is appropriate to the building and the setting. I want colours – and textiles, too – that come from the landscape around the house, the weather and the seasons. I think of the colour that I have used so far as a base for building up more colour. It's a bit like doing a painting really.'

The entire space – serene and simple as it is – suits its purpose perfectly: to act as a retreat, perhaps, but also as a place where Sebastian's work as an artist can constantly be refined.

ABOVE AND RIGHT There are more bedrooms here than it would seem at first sight: two double bedrooms, each with its own bathroom, one on the ground floor and one above, as well as a single bedroom and a bed on the upper gallery. Cleverly used to drape over beds and hang at the windows, Sebastian's collection of textiles come into their own in the bedrooms. All the bedrooms have floors of resin-coated concrete that has had pigment rubbed into it, and which gives the appearance of rich, old, polished tiles. In this bedroom, off the living area, the bed was designed by Sebastian.

LEFT The bedroom incorporates a bathing area. Against the Tuscan wardrobe leans a set of Chinese bamboo steps; the airy stools are in fact French luggage stands, and above the entrance to the washroom a golden sun of a lamp – 'Diosculo' from the 'Luci d'Ombra' collection by Benedetta Brunotti – gives off a soft background glow.

Casellacce had originally been rebuilt in the 1930s. 'We decided to demolish it and rebuild it in more fitting style,' explains Ilaria Miani, the owner, who is a designer in Rome. The interior is characterized by all-round elegance. Elegant may not seem the most appropriate word to describe a rural Italian country house, but to be elegant is to be refined and defined, to be edited and disciplined, and all these qualities are found at Casellacce. It is also extremely contemporary in feel; although often used pejoratively, the adjective contemporary is used here with a sense of admiration.

'In rebuilding the house, we kept in mind some elements of the original architecture – the central staircase, for example, and the kitchen, which retains the original heavily beamed ceiling – but the rest was laid out within the existing framework,' says Ilaria Miani. The kitchen was converted from what was formerly the stable building.

Ilaria designs furniture, which she sells in her Rome showroom, and, with the exception of a few family items, most of the pieces in the house are her work, from the sofas in the sitting room to some of the beds and the long bench in the entrance hall. She comments that the restoration of Casellacce has been what she calls an interesting synergy – 'not only using pieces from my existing range here, but

a haven of harmony

Casellacce is an invention – a fact that Ilaria Miani, well-known interior designer and owner of a Rome-based furnishing company, is proud to acknowledge, for it is an invention with charm and elegance, of a type not often seen in an ordinary country house.

ABOVE Casellacce offers spectacular views on every side. The house is filled with light, and the sleek lines of the pool seem to draw the eye towards the house, which, although rebuilt, looks as if it has never changed.

RIGHT There is a pleasure taken in functional objects, such as these hand-woven baskets, which have been displayed on shelves in an unused corner, allowing the shape and patterns of the baskets to be appreciated and admired.

THIS PAGE Although simply furnished and with little ornament, this sitting room is nevertheless a room of sophistication, anchored by the sofas designed by Ilaria Miani and cleverly covered with two jewel colours in linen from Ian Mankin, 'to mix and match', as Ilaria says. The vaulted brick ceiling tones with the wall colour – pigment added to plaster – and the oversized mirror gives added depth to the room.

also being able to test out new ideas that I have then been able to put into my future ranges.' Throughout the house, the plaster walls have been coloured with pigment while the plaster was still wet – a traditional method of adding colour to an interior, and a technique that is still as effective and eye-catching today as it ever was.

Ilaria is good at colour – very good – and she has cleverly used colour on the walls and in her choice of textiles, that work together in counterpoint. She has done this by keeping the colour of the walls muted and using fabric colour as accent: 'Every room of the house has a special view, and the landscape and light filling every window

OPPOSITE Converted from the original stable building, the kitchen is one of those wonderful rooms of which dreams are made. Everything has its place – wine bottles are stored within the depth of the wall above the window; and the old chimney breast is home to a contemporary fire, with an industrial cooking hob ranged on either side of it. Chairs in various colours relieve the otherwise neutral scheme.

ABOVE The grey plaster walls here and throughout the house are the backdrop for everything from fresh garden produce to the contrasting textures of wood and metal.

RIGHT At the other end of the kitchen is the dining area, where modular tables can be used in various configurations, depending on the occasion. The chestnut chairs were made by Miani after an old Polish design, and the iron lamps are from a range in her city showroom.

LEFT Several bedrooms lead off the first-floor corridor. The tufa-coloured walls make a backdrop for a series of Tuscan trunks painted in various washes. The beamed ceiling is made from local bricks in a distinctive pale terracotta.

BELOW The main bedroom has a beamed ceiling and a loft area above and behind the bed, whose design is based on a French campaign bed. The same tufa-coloured plaster walls are emphasized by pale grey door reveals.

RIGHT Basins in travertine marble stand on a locally made basalt base; the lampshades above the unit were designed by Ilaria Miani.

FAR RIGHT In another bedroom, a luxurious window seat has been built into an alcove flanked by cupboards with pedimented tops and interiors painted with beach-hut stripes. The chestnut floor is also painted – in matt grey.

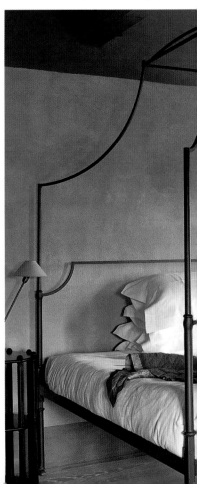

Every element has been carefully chosen, from the furniture to the fabrics, and every element is plainly and simply harmonious.

are the best pictures and the best light that you could have; for that reason I have kept the colour scheme for the walls and furniture very soft: grey for the ground floor and a sort of tufa [limestone] colour for the first floor.'

The fabrics that Ilaria chose for the house were an entirely different matter, however: 'It was in the textiles that I introduced strong colours: pink, orange, lilac, fuchsia and purple. I wanted them to cause surprise, give enjoyment, and add life and energy to everyday living. A cupboard can look very serious from the outside, but here, when you open it, you will find something unexpected – there will be coloured, painted stripes, or it will be lined

with a quilted fabric. A bed may be constructed to a simple design, but the sheets and covers should be sumptuous or colourful.'

In the restoration of Casellacce, Ilaria Miani has been inspired by the work of the late American artist and sculptor Donald Judd, who espoused the philosophy of 'empty volume'. She has consequently sought to keep the interior architecturally clean and completely devoid of clutter, with every piece of furniture thoughtfully placed.

It has personality, this house, and is comfortable with its simplicity; every element has been carefully chosen, from the furniture to the fabrics, and every element is plainly and simply harmonious.

understated grace

The Italian countryside is as varied as it is beautiful. Although there are areas that epitomize the traditional landscape known to admirers of Renaissance painting, other parts are very different. The Maremma is just such a distinct region, where the land itself is low, swampy almost, as it rolls down towards the sea.

The owner of this beautiful house in the Maremma, just outside the old hilltop town of Capalbio, is an interior designer who co-manages a gallery and shop called Contemporanea in the centre of Rome. Contemporanea specializes in the distinctive and modern, including witty creations by the likes of English designer Mark Brazier-Jones, known for his original ironwork pieces.

Grounded in a small grove of olives, the house stands square and confident in the flat landscape. It does not conform to the conventional idea of the Italian farmhouse. For one thing, it is not especially old – having been built in the 1950s – and, for another, it was not built for a farming family, but erected by the local council for farm workers to live in while they were draining the swamps of the Maremma, after which time they were able to work the land. Each family was granted a house with

THIS PAGE The dining room, which leads off the kitchen and is part of a new extension added about three years ago, has walls created by adding colour to a water base and applying the mixture to wet plaster. The table's base is by the British designer Mark Brazier-Jones.

Pale colour palettes veer towards the neutral, but with contrasts of texture and shade that soften what might otherwise be hard edges, with changes in floor surfaces and wall tones.

ABOVE A small study on the landing is decorated in the same clean style as the rest of the house; against a neutral, textured wall are small tables designed by Mark Brazier-Jones, whose work is sold in Contemporanea. The black-stained bookcase is made of chestnut.

RIGHT At the other end of the living room is a clutch of beautiful objects: the cabinet – in plastered wood – has doors made by Gennaro Avallone in plaster over canvas. On the cabinet next to an empty frame by the Japanese designer Mineko is a head cast by Oliviero Rinaldi. The white leather bench and cushions are from Contemporanea.

OPPOSITE In one corner of the living room, the soft hue of the French painted cabinet dating from the 18th century is emphasized by the pale travertine marble stairs that climb around it; the plaster fireplace in the foreground is a Contemporanea design.

4,000 square metres (4,780 square yards) of land. From these somewhat unpromising foundations, the interior designer from Rome has shaped a country residence that combines simplicity and stylish design with a complete lack of pretension.

As far as the exterior was concerned, it was important to the owner and her family that the restored house should be in keeping with the spirit of the surrounding area. Although they added a small wing to accommodate living and dining areas, in other respects, she says, 'We tried to leave the structure much as we found it, since the local architecture and profile is very low-key; we decorated the outside of the house in a way that, we hoped, would give the impression that it had simply evolved over the passage of time.'

Inside the house she was eager to create a look that was of the house and its history and yet was contemporary in feeling, using a combination of the past and the present. Elements of the past were chosen to reflect the history of the area, while elements of the present make themselves felt in the often quirky juxtaposition of objects that can be seen throughout the house. Architecturally, the

owner boldly decided to create a doorless enfilade between the downstairs rooms – a device that increases the sense of space while simultaneously retaining the notion of simple living and working areas. Upstairs, the master bedroom is a success story in miniature – a tiny room with just enough space for a bed; a door facing the bed opens to reveal a massive bathtub in a tiny cupboard. It is a witty reversal of the usual arrangement.

The decoration – which is so subtle as to be hardly designated as such – is what the owner calls 'minimalist baroque'. It is almost monastic in feel, but with an air of relaxed comfort – all very much in the style of the owner's gallery in Rome.

It is an attempt, and a triumphant one at that, to challenge the conventional idea of 'country style' and to create an informal, modern version of a comfortable rural interior.

In every room the colour palette is pale, veering towards the neutral, but with contrasts of texture and shade that soften the edges of what might otherwise be too hard-lined, with changes in floor surfaces and wall tones. Nothing has been done without a reason – from kitchen to bedrooms, every object, every detail, has been considered at length, every piece of furniture chosen with care. It represents, as the owner so accurately says, 'a new way to live in the countryside'.

ABOVE LEFT The master bedroom is stamped with the owner of Contemporanea's decorative signature: an inspirational combination of the past and present. In this room, the past is reflected in the old lace cushions and in the panelling, while modern design is represented in a bedside light by Mark Brazier-Jones.

ABOVE A hand-cut stone basin is offset by modern stainless-steel taps and a decorative mirror, complete with curlicues and flourishes.

OPPOSITE Glimpsed from the bedroom, the deep rounded bath, designed by Philippe Starck, stands firmly on a floor of whitewashed oak boards. Above the bath hangs a flamboyantly grand 19th-century French chandelier.

The word 'eclectic' is often used as a catch-all to describe a confusion of ideas and objects. But in Italian hands, the eclectic style is as precise as its dictionary definition – ideas 'borrowed from various sources' – and, in this case, borrowed in an educated manner and then put together again with discrimination, taste and, above all, wit.

eclectic

OPPOSITE In the hallway of La Querciola, a new simple set of stairs designed by Jean-Phillipe Gauvin rises through the centre of the house to connect the lower floor – which used to be the cow byre – with the upper living floor. Isabelle de Borchgrave's distinctive painting skills can be seen in the overall floral design of the open cupboard as well as in the broad stripes of subtle colour on the farthest wall.

RIGHT A loggia runs the length of the house; the brick arches have been half faced in plaster, and at one end steps lead to the upper portico. The soft-toned cushions on benches and chairs are covered in De Borchgrave fabrics.

BELOW In keeping with the calm atmosphere of the house, the large pool presides serenely over the unspoiled surrounding countryside.

a wreck restored

La Querciola is a house of surprises. At first glance it appears as if it has always been the way it is now. Built in the 17th century, it is clearly a little older than it once was, but seems to be a house that is ageing gracefully. In fact, nothing could be further from the truth.

When Isabelle and Werner de Borchgrave first came upon La Querciola, it was about as ruined as a house could be. Once the home of some 30 peasants, who lived on the first floor with their cattle ensconced in byres on the ground floor, it was, when they saw it, a derelict house on a rural estate of other equally derelict houses. It was so derelict in fact that the roof had caved in, crashing through the floors on its way to ground level.

The ambitious plan was to exchange the cows and the workers for four families, including the de Borchgraves. Each family would share the costs of the restoration and then use the place as a summer home. To achieve this end, Werner and Isabelle engaged architect Jean Philippe Gauvin, a man who shared their vision and, with them, was

'This type of house imposes on you what it already is,' says Werner. 'You don't want to intervene too much, and the proportions are so nice that you don't want to change them.'

OPPOSITE, ABOVE RIGHT A substantial hall leads off the kitchen, creating an airy open-plan space; painted in a subtle pale grey, the curves of the arch are highlighted with a darker grey stripe to emphasize the architectural contours.

OPPOSITE, LEFT AND BELOW RIGHT Once a cow byre, now a kitchen large enough for everyone, the room has been painted with soft, subtle colour with bright touches, such as the pink wooden cupboard.

keen to keep the original atmosphere and period of the house – for, as Werner says, 'This type of house imposes on you what it already is; you don't want to intervene too much, and the proportions are so nice that you don't want to change them.'

Like many farmhouses that originally combined both human and animal life, access to the first floor was gained only by external steps, so Gauvin designed a simple, narrow staircase to rise through the centre of the house; this, and the addition of a false light in the ceiling, effectively opened up a previously dead area, adding new space and life to the old building. On the first floor there were originally five rooms, heated by a large fireplace, where the farmers lived and slept; these were converted into bedrooms, as was space in the attic above, providing today a grand total of nine bedrooms, each with its own bathroom.

The vaulted cow byres on the ground floor were imaginatively converted by Gauvin and now have huge glass doors at either end, which add light as well as eliminating the difference between outside and in. One of the byres has been made into a big kitchen, with an oversized table and modern appliances along one wall; the other is a light-filled hall that leads out onto a long loggia. Although the ground floor is painted white, Isabelle, a noted

ABOVE In completely different mode to the rest of the house is a narrow sitting room decorated by Isabelle with many different motifs and designs. The background colour - a warm terracotta - is embellished with trompe l'oeil garlanded columns and different borders of intricate design. Benches are heaped high with cushions covered in some of de Borchgrave's fabrics. As elsewhere in the house, most of the furniture was found locally.

BELOW A simple, oversized fireplace, once the hearth around which the original occupants lived, dominates the upstairs sitting room. The walls are painted in a subtle combination – bands of yellow and ochre running around the room. A terracotta tiled floor and a large sofa covered in emerald-green linen make the whole room glow with light, and ensure that the room is as pleasing in winter as it is in summer.

RIGHT The upper loggia of the de Borchgrave house is a sanctuary of shaded calm.

OPPOSITE In this small bedroom, a delicate, gauzy trompe l'oeil curtain has been painted on the walls. It has been made to look more real by being taken around only a part of the room, and by the fact that in places the wall texture can be seen underneath.

artist, has hand-painted aspects of many of the rooms. The colours are memorable, and the subtle palette is the result of a happy circumstance. At nearby Arezzo, in the church of San Francesco, a work by Piero della Francesca was being restored with the help of scaffolding; Isabelle was therefore able to see the original colour close-up – 'nose to wall', as Werner says – and the results reflect this detailed observation. Many of the textiles were also hand-painted by Isabelle – she used a different colour palette in each of the rooms and added cushions that subtly emphasize the scheme.

All the furniture was chosen for its suitability within these large spaces: some of it comes from the market at Arezzo, other pieces were originally found in Indonesia. 'Everything had to be big – the scale of the building is huge,' says Werner

Outside, on a coloured cement terrace, a long pool gives views over the hills, with a vine-covered pergola to one side; one could ask for little more.

RIGHT In the sheltered garden, Marina has kept the scheme simple, adding many more roses to those already there and planting regional species such as lavender and rosemary.

beyond the rainbow

Walking into Marina Pignatelli's Tuscan farmhouse is like walking through a rainbow into whatever may lie beyond; every room glows with clear colours, infused with light, cloaking the walls with tones that imperceptibly blend with the next. But it was not always like this.

LEFT From the farmhouse there are views over a great swathe of countryside that appears almost uninhabited. The swimming pool in the foreground of this tranquil scene was designed to appear to overflow into the landscape beyond, and is bordered by irregularly cut slabs of pinky white stone – *pietra di Trani* from Puglia. The pool walls have been painted a pale pink shade to echo the colour of the stone, giving an almost translucent cast to the water.

Marina Pignatelli found the house five years ago. Her origins are Tuscan and she had been keen to buy a house in the region. 'I had been searching in Val D'Orcia and the surrounding area for more than two years, helped by some good friends who had discovered this incredible spot years ago.'

The 'incredible spot' is a wild, unspoiled part of Tuscany, in the province of Siena. Marina's house is backed by oak woods that come right up to the edge of the house, while in front the wide, open landscape, reminiscent of a 15th-century Sienese painting, stretches to encompass Mount Amiata and the Rocca di Radicofani. As Marina says, 'As far as the eye can go, there is no 20th century to be seen.'

As luck would have it, the original farmhouse's brick floors were still in place, as were the doors, beams and an open fireplace.

The farmhouse dates from the 17th century and, unusually, the structure had already been restored by an English owner; Marina's role, as she saw it, was to do the interior decoration, landscape the garden and make a swimming pool.

It was important to her that the house should be cosy and comfortable – Tuscan winters can be cold – so she decided to keep the oldest part, on the upper floor, as it was when the farmers were still in residence. As luck would have it, the original brick floors were still in place, as were the doors, beams and an open fireplace. This part of the house has now been arranged to make three large bedrooms, three bathrooms, a living room and a small kitchen.

The ground floor, once the domain of the animals and used for the most part as a stable, has been turned into a huge living-and-everything-else room, a large kitchen and a dining room – as well as two more bedrooms and a bathroom.

'I wanted a natural and comfortable house that was not contrived – a place where I could gather my thoughts and find myself. I wanted it to look like me, and that is why I combined a traditional, simple countryside style with an oriental look.' Marina is a traveller and she bought many of the pieces in the house during her travels around the world. She is particularly attached to the Middle East and India, and has found that Tuscan farmhouse furniture

OPPOSITE The design of the kitchen focuses on simple ideas executed in a sophisticated manner. Open shelves and wooden cupboards are used for storage, and the travertine sink is a modern take on the traditional stone sink. A set of old German scales combines the virtues of practicality and display.

BELOW A baker's credenza or sideboard – that most useful, as well as decorative, piece of furniture – separates the kitchen part of the room from the dining area. This one is a 19th-century piece made in Treviso.

RIGHT Since it was important to keep the kitchen warm and comfortable in winter, the fireplace was central to the whole room. The walls have been coloured by Marina in the traditional manner, with hand-mixed colour; the rose colour on the upper walls contrasts with a deep green band painted up to dado level.

LEFT In the largest sitting room, once the main stables, an old credenza from Naples and a Syrian mirror are placed against an ochre-coloured wall. In lieu of a wooden door frame, a painted border runs around the door and around the base at skirting level.

Learning the fresco technique from a Tuscan artisan, Marina mixed four basic hues with water and clay to get the shades she wanted.

LEFT The seating in this sitting room is simple and very effective. It consists of large, low wooden bases with firm canvas seat cushions, on top of which are piles of assorted cushions in bolster and rectangular shapes, covered in Indian fabrics. A Turkish kelim in front of the fire is highlighted by two large Indian lanterns.

mixes well with country furniture from other worlds: 'There are the 19th-century Chinese peasants' wedding cabinets, the ornamental iron beds I bought in Greece and the tea tables I found in Turkey.' The carpets were also bought in exotic places such as Syria, Turkey and Tibet after many hours of bargaining over apple tea and shish kebab.

India was the source for most of the textiles in the house – light transparent organza saris, and muslins for the curtains and beds; silks for cushions, and linens and raw cottons for the sofas. 'For the big yellow living room, I was inspired by the caravanserai of Syria and made huge long sofas simply from wooden bases along the wall, with large canvas seat cushions and lots more cushions on top,' says Marina. From Tibet she adapted the nomad tradition of hanging fabrics over a door, which adds warmth to the rooms in winter.

Marina likes natural colours and desired to use traditional painting methods, so she learned the fresco technique from a Tuscan artisan and made the colours herself, using four basic hues and mixing them with water and clay to create the shades she wanted. The main room is ochre; the kitchen and dining room are pink with a green

ABOVE The elaborate 'Pastorale' iron bed in this bedroom dates from the 17th century. Also known as a bishop's bed, it has two curved rods (with a bar across) at the foot designed to hold ceremonial clothing. Low iron pendant lights hang on either side of the bed. Walls the colour of a blood orange, a deep pink Indian bedspread and antique linen complete the picture.

ABOVE RIGHT AND OPPOSITE Where straw hats now hang from a metal stand, hams used to hang in winter, ready to be eaten. Now, the pale grey-blue of the walls and the gauze bed curtains make this a very feminine room.

RIGHT The unlined sheer curtains are chosen to reinforce the colours of the corridor walls.

skirting board. The main bedrooms are pale blue and the iron-bedded room is orange with a grey skirting board. 'These intense, brilliant but natural colours are ideal in a house like this.' The natural concept is continued in the garden, where Marina added to the existing dog roses with many more roses – over 130 varieties, new and old – as well as lavender, rosemary and other regional species.

The swimming pool, which overlooks the valley, is a wonderfully tranquil spot. 'I spent two months overseeing every detail. The idea was to choose the widest possible view so that the overflow would seem to vanish into nowhere. As a border for the pool, I chose *pietra di Trani*, large, irregularly cut stones from Puglia; their whiteish pink colour made me decide to paint the inside of the pool the same tone. The result is fantastic – the transparency and colour of the water are truly beautiful.' As indeed is the whole domain.

RIGHT Built in the mid-20th century, the house – a former home for several families of peasants working on the estate – needed a new roof and various essential additions. The setting and the landscape were the departure points for the interior and exterior decoration; here a sunny terrace leads onto a grassed area with wide views of the landscape beyond.

LEFT Evident from this table arrangement is Gabriella's understanding and professional use of colour. The strong vivid hues reflect her personality; dressing the table is a wide runner from her collection of oriental textiles, which complements the cheerful ceramic dishes.

a traveller's tale

Much of Gabriella Abbado's working life has been spent in the world of design. She is also an inveterate traveller, absorbing design and ideas wherever she goes, so it is no surprise that her country house in Italy is both assured and simple – a confident statement and collection of the pieces and looks that really please her.

Gabriella Abbado's long involvement with design spans both fashion and interiors. During the 1960s she worked with such fashion names as Oleg Cassini and the inimitable Anna Piaggi, and on the interiors side she worked in London in the 1980s with John Howard, designing furniture. All those influences were brought to bear on the restoration and decoration of her Italian country home.

When Gabriella bought the house in 1994, it was – like so many buildings of this type – a ruin. Built in 1938 on the Engebels' estate, which had been established in 1910, it had originally been a farmhouse for several peasant families. 'The house was a ruin standing on very rough stony ground. I

restored it, keeping the original structure and proportions, but putting on a new roof and opening up windows that had been filled in, and installing a bathroom – obviously a necessity,' says Gabriella. She wanted to use materials for the restoration that were sympathetic to the area and the local countryside, materials that were 'solid rather than precious'. Happily, she was able to preserve much of the original building materials, although some of the floors had to be replaced.

Gabriella wanted to make the interior comfortable but restrained, which meant preserving the natural simplicity of the interior spaces, rather than imposing a contrived design-fuelled 'simple look' on what was already there. It should also, she felt, be furnished with 'simplicity and love'. Gabriella has collected 20th-century furniture for many years, and she saw that her new house would be the perfect home

for many of the pieces. 'When I saw the quality of the space here, I realized I would be able to use a number of pieces of furniture that I had put in store and that were part of a past that was very dear to me; they were all of a style that was very popular in the 1970s and obviously I chose pieces that were suitable for a country house.'

The result is an extraordinary success. Solid, chunky pieces of furniture fill the rooms and emphasize the basic architecture, the curved arches, the heavy beams. There are also many decorative objects and works of art from Africa and Asia, because Gabriella loves the forms found in the artistic expression of those cultures. Throughout the house is colour, chosen by Gabriella in an artistic and unusual way: 'I believe that every house has a colour destiny, which comes from outside – from the history of the local village, the setting

LEFT A spacious kitchen and dining area has been created from what were once the stables. Wood predominates here. A Tuscan shop counter makes an effective work surface, and the room is lit with a large metal pendant light – an iconic design of the 1970s by Flos.

ABOVE On the kitchen shelves is a collection of French pottery from the Luberon and Burgio plates from Sicily. The baskets are locally made.

OPPOSITE, LEFT The library end of the large living room features a practical and beautiful table designed by Muramo Palma, which was commissioned by Gabriella in 1974. The low-slung leather chaise longue was designed by Bellini in the early 1970s.

OPPOSITE, RIGHT At another end of the large living room, the fireplace makes a striking focus. On the mantelpiece is a pair of French candlesticks, based on the female form. The iron coffee table was designed by Gabriella.

'I believe every house has a colour destiny, which comes from outside – from the history of the local village, the setting and landscape, to the variety of light throughout the day.'

OPPOSITE In the master bedroom, a fine grey line has been painted around the wall at picture-rail height, separating the lower pale blue section from the pale cream upper section. The bed is from Kashmir – and Gabriella has added a narrow metal frame between the posts for a linen hanging; the bedcover is also from Kashmir, and over the bedhead is draped an ornate piece of cutwork linen. The bench at the end of the bed was found locally.

LEFT Also in the master bedroom, an antique Tuscan cupboard with its original paint stands next to a Chinese stepladder; on a rug from Morocco is a woven cane daybed from India.

ABOVE AND ABOVE LEFT In the master bathroom, basins set into a wooden top are lit with art deco lamps dating – like the wooden mirror frame – from the 1930s. On either side of the mirror are groups of tiles from Seville.

and landscape, to the variety of light throughout the day; the strong colours reflect my personality, but also correspond to the relative harshness of the surrounding countryside.' Much of the colour comes in shots supplied through textiles collected on her travels. 'From the simplest to the most luxurious, textiles always have a story to tell.'

The house changes its look according to the time of year, for Gabriella believes that a living environment should renew itself with the seasons, and that colours and fabrics should be rich and warm in winter, cooler and simpler in summer. 'Fabrics and light determine the balance of the interior decoration,' she says. 'As a consequence, my homes have a series of "outfits" depending on the seasons. You could say that the house has its own wardrobe.'

a castle in Chianti

Over its 800-year-life, Castel Ruggero, in the Chianti region, has been through several different incarnations. Built in the 13th century as a monastery, where wine was made, it was turned into a fortified castle in the 15th century. By the time the family of artist Camilla d'Afflitto, the present owner, bought it, some centuries later, the need for fortified buildings was past, and Camilla and her sisters grew up there in tranquillity.

When Camilla inherited Castel Ruggero in 2001, she wanted to make changes to the interior. Every generation has its own way of living, and to her the house seemed oppressive and dark. Her desire was, she says, 'to return life to the house in a way that reflects my own artistic and living experience'. So she began extensive restorations – and the end was restorative rather than reconstructive, for the building remains entirely original, as it always was, and the work has been of renewal rather than replacement, of burnishing rather than bashing.

She decided not to alter in any major way the layout of the two floors. On the ground floor there are two living rooms, one larger than the other, and

ABOVE The winter sitting room: with Roberto Gerosa, Camilla d'Afflitto has covered the 1950s chairs and sofa with witty combinations of silks and velvets. The antique Persian rug, from which the furnishing colours were taken, was collected by Camilla's Turkish grandfather. The floor lamp is by Gerosa, and a lamp with a Venini glass base sits on the table.

LEFT The exterior of Castel Ruggero has changed little over the centuries, through its incarnations from wine-producing monastery to fortified castle to family home.

RIGHT A long hallway is used as an additional sitting room with a quantity of comfortable chairs and sofas, upholstered with imaginative flair, to accommodate Ruggero's many guests. The lamps and wall lights are again by Gerosa.

LEFT The emerald-green tiles in this bathroom are the original mosaic tiles installed in the 1950s. Camilla has reinforced their decorative appeal by covering the remainder of the wall with sponged bands of emerald-green paint.

BELOW AND RIGHT Leading from the mosaic bathroom is the master bedroom – a hybrid of a room that is hard to date. The silk bedspread is made from fabric by Scalamandre, which Camilla bought in New York. A 1950s chair has been covered with a cotton fabric from the same period, and the bedside lamp, which echoes the room's witty style, is by Roberto Gerosa. Above the long line of fitted wardrobes is a collection of 1950s ceramics.

what was a billiard room is used as an occasional dining room. Next to that is a room that was once blocked off, but which she has re-opened and turned into a kitchen. Upstairs on the first floor there is a further sitting room, a study and eight bedrooms, each with its own bathroom.

Throughout the house, the original floors remain, and these form the underpinning for the whole decorative approach. As Camilla says, 'The original floors are one of the most beautiful features of the house, both in terms of their colour and patina, as well as the warmth they create in every room.'

With this solid architectural and decorative base as a starting point, she could work towards her objective, which had always been to combine the traditional furniture of her childhood with her own collections of both decorative art and textiles.

Camilla took stock of the existing furniture, sold the heavier and more ponderous pieces, and cleared the rooms of all the existing decorative objects, putting them into cupboards to be re-evaluated and reintroduced over time in different contexts. 'In this way, I have achieved a harmony between my past and my present – and the soul of the house continues to grow and change,' she says.

Then came the time for Camilla to introduce her own collections, particularly her collection of Italian vases, which she had begun to put together when she was in her twenties. She also has a large and varied collection of textiles, which she has collected all her life, and which includes Italian, American and oriental pieces. All these she has placed around the house, combining West with East and old with new in a completely original way.

The architect Roberto Gerosa has contributed enormously to the restoration project, adding lamps and sofas, and introducing colour contrasts and combinations that are witty and eccentric.

The final result is an interesting, unique house: 'I don't enjoy the dark, lifeless, boring interiors that you sometimes find in Italian country houses,' says Camilla. 'I have tried to create a home which is the antithesis of that style – a home that reflects my love and passion for colour and light, as well as illustrating my respect for all the artists whose work is represented throughout the house.'

To Camilla, Castel Ruggero seemed oppressive and dark. Her desire was 'to return life to the house in a way that reflects my own artistic and living experience'. So the restoration work has been of renewal rather than replacement, of burnishing rather than bashing.

ABOVE Once the girls' bathroom, this room was decorated in the 1950s by Camilla's mother and still retains its charming flowery wallpaper. Camilla has painted the pink dressing table and chair to tone with the original scheme.

RIGHT The hallway outside the bathroom has been painted in shades of blue running through to grey, applied in broad horizontal stripes. The tiled floor – which is original, like all the floors in the house – is part of the decorative scheme.

OPPOSITE In this light bedroom the furniture, which came originally from the servants' wing of the house, has been painted in ice-cream colours by Camilla. The pieces of decorative glass are by Venini.

LEFT In the study within the main living room, everything from bookcases to desk to windows is painted in soft greens and greys. The lampshade is by Gerosa.

ABOVE As it changes from work area to sitting area, the room is a comfortable mixture of the old and the new, the simple and the grand.

RIGHT Kelims and covers in ethnic colours and patterns are draped over the furniture; antique sconces reflect the washed-out eau-de-nil of the walls.

simply grand

Teresa Ginori's house is a beguiling mix of the grand and the very simple – an unexpected combination in a small house that, from the outside at least, is not immediately striking as a building of distinction.

When Teresa first discovered the house, she was far from impressed. 'I fell in love with the property rather than the house,' she says. 'The land was hilly, partly wood, partly grass, and with huge wild hydrangea bushes growing everywhere. The house itself was ugly – but, because it had no personality, I thought it would be easy to give it some.'

That was in 2001, and it took Teresa a year to transform it into what she now calls her 'nest'. The architect Robert Gerosa, who is a friend, helped on

the interior and another friend, Nicolò Mori, worked with her on the garden. Unusually, she decided to put the bedrooms in the basement: 'I thought the low ceilings would keep the bedrooms cool, so in both rooms I installed large French windows that open onto a part of the garden that's full of apple trees, and a new floor made of unpolished offcuts of white Carrara marble.'

On the ground floor is the sitting room, one side of which acts as her study or office, and on the other side, close to the kitchen, stands the dining table. The kitchen itself is a pleasantly old-fashioned room. 'I don't like technical spaces,' says Teresa. 'Every room is a place that needs to be cosy, that needs a "heart", so to me a room is a room, and bathrooms and kitchens I decorate with

ABOVE The other main room in Teresa Ginori's house is the kitchen – part cooking space and part comfortable eating area. Like other rooms in the house, it is furnished in a mix of styles and periods, and includes an elaborate Venetian chandelier from Teresa's family home.

RIGHT Outside, on the deep porch, is an eccentric set of Austrian deer-horn furniture – including a twisted wreath of horns from which are hung assorted coloured tea lights. The porch acts almost as another room, adding dimension and space to the whole house.

LEFT AND RIGHT Other unusual yet entirely fitting pieces of furniture in the kitchen include the oversized credenza, found in a French pharmacy, which is the perfect cupboard for storing all the china and glass. An inspired choice for kitchen chairs are the painted iron chairs from India; the bright and cheerful colour of the tulips is echoed in the red stripes of the practical and simple curtains that run the length of the cooking and preparation side of the kitchen. Even the cooker hood is brought into the decorative scheme, acting as another surface on which to display decorative china.

FAR LEFT AND LEFT The wall behind the bath in the master bathroom is painted a pinky red, inspired by the changing tones of the hydrangeas in the garden; the colour was hand-painted and then resin-coated. The twin basins are set in black Carrara marble, cut to echo the curved lines of the wooden base; above is a 19th-century faux bamboo mirror.

OPPOSITE AND BELOW LEFT The reading corner in the master bedroom is dominated by a cement fireplace, decorated with a collection of early 19th-century Italian ceramics; on a Moroccan rug, low seating cushions have been covered with fabric offcuts. The red lampshade was adapted from a French mosquito-net holder designed to hang above a bed.

the same spirit as any other room.' Throughout the house there are pieces of interesting furniture and unexpected colour. 'I like eccentric old furniture because it has a story to tell. I admire the wit and creativity of craftsmen and the emotions they can transmit through their work. I like any style, as long as it's not "heavy" or too grand.'

Teresa had a particular aim in mind in choosing colours. 'Normally I believe that a house inspires you to find the right colours,' she says, 'but, since this one needed personality, I decided that I would pay homage to the hydrangeas outside that had impressed me so much.'

On one flank of the house, she constructed a portico with long wooden steps extending along its entire length, which act as seats, and beyond the house Nicolò Mori has helped her to create what she describes as a 'harmoniously untidy garden'. The space incorporates existing chestnut trees and fig trees as well as the famous hydrangeas, set off by other, differently coloured species to produce a veritable paintbox of blooms.

In Italian decorative terms at least, traditional is the opposite of boring. Traditional rural style, as practised by the owners and designers featured in this book, appreciates the tried, the tested, the best of what has gone before, and puts it all together in a way that is absolutely of our time.

traditional

LEFT The farmhouse and garden were rebuilt from a former working farm, which once had a full complement of stables, barns and pigsties.

OPPOSITE The lovely vaulted ceiling of the kitchen gives it a grace and lightness not often seen in such buildings; the arches separate the cooking area from the dining space, which is simply furnished with a long table made by Piet Hein Eek and chairs from Indonesia.

BELOW The kitchen area has two sinks, the smaller surrounded by hand-made Sicilian tiles, the larger made to measure from stone. Above the large sink is a 19th-century Tuscan cupboard, used to store plates and dishes.

sanctuary near Siena

When the de Loozes first saw the early 19th-century building near Siena, it was like many other long-abandoned Tuscan farmhouses, except that it was a lot larger than most others of its kind, even boasting its own small chapel. They bought it on a whim, deciding within 24 hours that it was the house for them.

Le Porciglia is a long, low, stone farmhouse outside Siena – but such a basic description does not at all convey the distinctive, unique personality of the house, or explain why it made such a strong initial impression on interior decorator Simone de Looze and her husband, its current owners.

Having made their decision to buy Le Porciglia, the de Loozes contacted the English designer Anthony Collett of Collett–Zarzycki to help them make sense of the space architecturally. Noted for his cool, clean approach to architectural and interior design, Collett has a house of his own in Tuscany that reflects his design principles. With the added help of an Italian architect, the trilingual Carlos Rex – the only one who was able to organize and deliver the many permits that were needed – they worked out a scheme that would make the best use of the 'rather ungainly' 1,000 square metres (10,800 square feet) of space. (In

ABOVE Hanging from the beams beyond the balustraded gallery in this double-height living room, a 19th-century French chandelier from a hotel in the south of France swings in front of one of the bedrooms.

RIGHT The large living room, decorated in pale neutral tones, has subtle architectural interest in the ceiling, where the design between the white-painted beams was copied from a church in Perugia. The striking 18th-century fireplace is faced by two high-backed Dutch chairs from the same period, and the pair of sofas are covered in unobtrusive white linen, allowing the many decorative pieces to take centre stage.

ABOVE Along one wall of the generously proportioned living room is a table covered with a fabric from India. It holds a surprising mixture of objects. In the centre is a crude model of the Archangel Gabriel next to a Cretan dish and a heap of old French boules; on either side, two tall candlesticks have been turned into lamps, and an African carved wooden dog stands alone. As if this were not enough, the display also includes an item of 19th-century fencing armour and, on the wall, an African ceremonial headdress.

addition to the chapel, there were stables, pigsties and barns.) The de Loozes wanted to create a house that was comfortable and friendly but with enough room and space for everyone to enjoy.

The eventual design featured a house with four bedrooms and an adjoining guest cottage in what had originally been the hay barn. There would have been more than four bedrooms, had not one of the owners' more unusual ideas been to create an airy, light, double-height living room in the main house, a room that soars up to the old beams; it includes a 19th-century chandelier that came from a hotel

in the south of France. Facing onto this space are the remaining bedrooms, one with an iron balcony overlooking the central space, the others leading out onto a balustraded gallery, salvaged from a 20th-century Italian theatre that burnt down. It is dramatic – and certainly not what you might expect to find within the walls of a Tuscan farmhouse.

The restoration was not carried out at great speed. In fact, Simone says, it took five years. But five years gives plenty of time to get things right, to reflect and sometimes rethink – and the result will almost always be better than a job done in haste.

ABOVE Simone collects country furniture from all over Europe. On top of a 17th-century cupboard from the Italian region of Le Marche, which still retains its original colour, are pots from Puglia. To make the floor, Simone used new terracotta tiles turned upside down and set in beige cement.

RIGHT The gallery in the living room is fitted with balustrading that once formed the balcony of an Italian theatre, burnt down in the 1920s.

OPPOSITE Simone covered the tall bedheads of these old iron beds with red fabric and added narrow canopies to make dramatic frames.

As well as being an interior decorator, Simone is an antiques dealer, as was her mother before her, and her passion for rural and country style goes back a very long way, so she was definite about what she wanted. 'When I was still a little girl, I started to collect clippings from interiors magazines, and over all the years my taste for the things I'd like in a southern European country house has not changed.'

Simone wanted to use a neutral palette. 'I don't like the use of much colour in rustic-style houses; the objects and furniture all have a story to tell, and they do that better against a neutral background.'

The neutral background was intended to set off many pieces of rustic antique furniture – Italian yes, but also Dutch and French. 'Like my mother, I've developed a liking for country furniture that literally falls apart.' If that is the case, the various fragile pieces must have been very well repaired; there is little evidence in the elegantly furnished rooms of make-do-and-mend. Perhaps this reflects Simone's other skill – the arrangement of rooms, the most important attribute of a good interior decorator. As Simone says, 'As an antiques dealer, one learns that decorating is all about the right objects put together in

THIS PAGE In one of the striking bathrooms, the marble bathtub, looking like something found in an ancient Roman villa, was in fact made in Livorno in the mid-18th century. The ornate tin mirror also comes from Livorno, but dates from a century later, and the cabinet below is also Italian.

LEFT Built in along the length of the bath is a pair of alcoves for storing soap and potions; they are finished in early 20th-century tiles, hand-made and hand-painted in Sicily.

BELOW The simple style of this bedroom is typical of Simone de Looze's brand of interior decoration. A large but unadorned bed has no bedhead; instead, she has hung behind the bed an Indian textile consisting of a motif of cypress trees set against a white background – a copy of the Punjabi original in the Victoria and Albert Museum in London. The bedcover is also white, with a naïve rendition of fruit and flowers.

the right way. Even a "wrong" room can be made "right" if it has fantastic stuff in it.' Apart from the confident design of the internal space, there are other architectural elements that catch the eye, such as the floors, particularly a floor that looks like a wide-spaced chequerboard of old terracotta tiles. Simone designed this with new tiles that are simply turned upside down and set into cement that has been tinted beige. 'It was a dream to experiment with the floors in Le Porciglia. On this floor we put old or new *cotto* tiles into coloured cement, but the variations are endless.' In keeping with the cool feel of the house, textiles are not a major feature of the design, but pretty pieces crop up everywhere, many collected by Simone from all over the world.

It is a lovely house – calm and generous, grand in its concept of space, but comfortable in its use of it. It is Simone's version of Italian country style, which involves, she says, 'No chintz curtains, no hunting prints, and never, never, modern bathrooms.'

RIGHT Once a resting place for weary pilgrims, Buon Riposo has again become a place where guests can stop and relax under shade-giving trees, relishing the peace of the timeless landscape.

BELOW AND RIGHT The original role of Buon Riposo as a staging post for coaches taking pilgrims on to the holy city of Rome is evident in its series of linked courtyards. Ilaria Miani and her husband were careful to respect the different architectural ages of Buon Riposo and to restore it with sensitivity and care.

a pilgrims' staging post

When, in the late 1980s, Ilaria Miani and her husband found the house known as Buon Riposo, it was nothing like it appears here. In fact it was more or less a ruin – one of the many ruins that could then be found scattered through this part of rural Italy.

The Via Francigena was the great medieval road that led to Rome from France, and the Orcia valley was dotted with more than 20 resting places for devout pilgrims on their journey to the Holy City. As Ilaria Miani and her husband, Giorgio, began to dig about and explore the ruin that they had bought, they found evidence to suggest that Buon Riposo had once been something more than simply a peasants' dwelling – that on this site there had once stood one of the pilgrims' houses of rest.

As the Mianis began to work on the house, the strata of centuries of life began to emerge, yielding clues to the building's age and use, clues like the very old floor tiles found in one part of the house that were inscribed 'Fabio Carli, 1560' – the name of a local brick furnace of the period. Eventually they deduced that Buon Riposo had indeed been a dwelling in the 16th century, and had been added

OPPOSITE To connect a reading area with the sitting room beyond, Ilaria designed a passage lined with book shelves on both sides and around the entrance.

LEFT New ceiling beams were built to recreate and replace the originals in the sitting room. Since the original ceiling was quite low, the height was increased by sinking the sitting-room floor.

BELOW LEFT The kitchen sink and worktop were made from the stone Marmo di Santa Fiore at Siena and are set on whitewashed plain wooden cupboard doors.

to in the 18th century, and partially restored in the early 20th century. It became clear that, were they to restore it anew, they needed to take its past into account and reflect in its restoration the different periods of its long life. 'As it was so obviously an ancient house,' says Ilaria, 'we sought to bring it back to what must have been its perfect simplicity.'

With this end in mind, they researched all the antiques dealers within a range of 150 kilometres (90 miles), visiting them in a quest for the most authentic materials – 'searching always for the right tiles, the right bricks and the right beams'.

Luck played its part in the restoration. At nearby Villa La Foce, owned by Marchesa Iris Origo, there was a fresco that depicted Buon Riposo in the 19th century, which showed enough contemporary detail to give the Mianis a start, and the confidence that their restorative instincts were correct.

Furniture is always something to be thought about with care in a restoration project of this kind, and the mix of furniture here is unusual. 'Actually, it is a period pastiche,' says Ilaria. 'I inherited some pieces from my grandmother and more from a family house in Cortina d'Ampezzo. My grandmother collected 19th-century furniture, and the Cortina house had been built in the 1940s by Tullio Rossi, a renowned architect of the day who designed all the furniture for the house as well, so that was

that. But Buon Riposo is large and still more furniture was needed, so I began to design my own beds, tables and chairs to fill the gaps. I made the furniture to be both functional and flexible – often a modular piece that I could use in different ways in the same room, or move from one room to another. I like to change my houses according to the mood of the moment, and I enjoy experimenting.

But I have to admit that the consequence of combining furniture from all these different periods really is a pastiche!' A pastiche it may be, but it is far from contrived. As Ilaria says, 'What I wanted to avoid was falling into the trap of creating fake rustic decoration – trying to reinvent a peasant style that, in Tuscany at any rate, never existed.' In fact, the result is a pleasing timelessness.

OPPOSITE In the dining room, in front of a set of table and chairs designed by the renowned architect Tullio Rossi in the 1940s, and adorned with candlesticks by Ilaria Miani, is a large mural by Maurizio Ligas showing the houses of the Val d'Orcia, with Siena in the top left-hand corner.

LEFT A set of white-painted wooden pegs has been fixed beneath a shelf, where they are used to hang towels and bathroom pieces.

ABOVE LEFT The storage alcove above the bath has been outlined with a broad band of white paint, making a subtle contrast with the cream-painted plaster wall.

ABOVE Seen from the bathroom, against the same cream plaster wall, and on a terracotta tiled floor, a rather heavy antique wooden bed has been simplified by Ilaria and washed white. Like other decorative elements, the colours throughout Buon Riposo have been kept very simple.

a decorative feast

A successful blend of the traditional and the new is always hard to achieve, but for Piero Castellini Baldissera the genre holds no fears. An expert in the art of interior decoration, he is adept at mixing scale and shape, colour and texture into a harmonious whole, and one that is always in perfect taste.

Piero Castellini Baldissera is one of the masters of Tuscan restoration. Whether it is because of his understanding of the landscape and the place that each house holds in the countryside, or whether it is because of his love of traditional materials and colours, the houses that he brings back to life are always places of pleasurable calm and relaxation.

Lavacchio is in the middle of Tuscany – a long low farmhouse surrounded by a verdant orchard in some amazingly beautiful countryside. From the outside, the house is unassuming, but once you are inside all is surprising. As is so often the case in this part of Italy, the house was not always quite as comfortable as it is today, having been originally a

THIS PAGE AND OPPOSITE The long low sitting room is dominated by a commanding stone fireplace surmounted by an evocative landscape. The room is a perfect example of harmony and scale. Colours, though muted, are never bland, and are actually very varied – they reflect the colours of the earth and sun, and every surface seems to meld gracefully into the next. The textures are equally compatible – stone, wood, plaster, tiles and textiles sit happily together. While chairs and sofas are covered in different patterns and designs, the windows are left uncompromisingly bare.

home for cows, and when Piero Castellini Baldissera first saw it, it was abandoned and uninhabitable, even by cows.

How things change! In his restoration of the building, Piero has cleverly kept all the best things about the house – its soul, the walls and floors, beams and windows, and worked around them, adding all the elements necessary to make it a living, comfortable house.

Inside the house all is warm and welcoming; textures and materials are of paramount importance – the central rooms have heavily beamed ceilings and the tiled floors have been restored and sealed. Throughout the house, furniture is

chosen with care and the details – always an area in which Piero excels – complement the furnishings with aplomb.

In the long living room with its low, beamed ceiling, the focal point is a fireplace that is surprisingly smart – not a huge chimney piece in which food was once prepared, but an urban sophisticated piece that stands in contrast to the rustic surroundings. The chairs also are loose-covered and comfortable; library chairs, chairs that are used for reading and relaxing. This is the secret of Piero's style, the ability to create a sophisticated interior that is yet completely in keeping with the house's position and architectural style.

LEFT One of Piero's secrets is not to overcomplicate matters, and there is never too much of anything. In this bathroom, the bath is fixed in the centre of the room with a double curtain around it; although there are few modern gadgets, a comfortable chair and a practical towel rail are placed conveniently near to hand.

ABOVE AND OPPOSITE The bedroom is as simple as the bathroom. An ornate traditional iron bed has curtains only, rather than the addition of a canopy, which would have hidden the curved arches of iron. No rug is necessary. There are simply two tall reading lights and, at the foot of the bed, a comfortable stool.

Colour and its use are Piero's other most powerful tools – whether they are warm, earthy tones or cool, refreshing shades, he applies them with confidence. Sometimes a colour is textured, looking like the plaster itself, and sometimes it is applied in a pattern – more often than not, a broad stripe, one of his decorative signatures and used on both walls and furniture.

The secret here is both the width of the stripe and the fact that it is always hand-painted, which gives it a depth and a delightful unevenness, in keeping with the relaxed surroundings. The stripes are sometimes in strong contrast and sometimes in complementary shades of a single colour; they are always effective. This theme of stripes continues onto the fabrics that he employs – curtains and furnishings are all subject to stripes of different colours and depths – a timeless decorating secret.

Piero's other most distinctive skill lies in his attention to decorative detail. He takes enormous pleasure in the arrangement of pictures, objects and decorative pieces, using them to create tableaux and conversation pieces on surfaces and walls throughout the house. The result is a house that is both comfortable and interesting – a true gentleman's country retreat.

Inside, all is warm and welcoming; textures and materials are paramount – the central rooms have heavily beamed ceilings and the tiled floors have been restored and sealed.

OPPOSITE One of the horses owned by Idarica Gazzoni and her husband Piero Prinetti stands in the courtyard of the 18th-century farmhouse that the couple have restored over the past 15 years.

ABOVE AND RIGHT Throughout the house are signs of Piero's passion for horses and horse-riding. The hallway, decorated in deep prune and terracotta, is filled with riding boots and jackets.

the effects of paint

Idarica Prinetti is a talented decorative artist – so, when she and her husband, the head of a large advertising agency in Milan, found this former peasants' house in the Monferrato, about an hour from Milan, it was only natural that she would elect to decorate the house herself.

As far as the decoration was concerned, Idarica had to be patient. The first task was to make the house habitable, and it was not easy. Previously owned by a farmer, when the Prinettis found it, it had been completely abandoned. Outside, there was no garden, and very little landscape – the farmer had cut down the surrounding trees. Inside, it was equally bleak. There was no electricity, no water and consequently no bathrooms. Even worse, during the farmer's tenure he had attempted partially to restore the building and had replaced much of the original building materials with concrete.

The outlook was not encouraging, but energy and enthusiasm carried the Prinettis forward. They bored for water and made wells, and then planted the garden and started to restore the house.

ABOVE On a table is part of Idarica's Indian ring collection from Jaipur; the rubies, emeralds and sapphires inspired the colour that she used in the decoration of the house.

RIGHT The living room was once a farm store. Its original vaulted ceiling was sanded and sealed and now frames the far end of the room.

OPPOSITE At the other end of the room are the dining table and bookcases. Much of the furniture was found in local shops; the wire chair is a Cappellini design. Evidence of Idarica's travels are found in the kelim from Turkey and the overhead lantern from Zanzibar.

The ground floor of the house had been mostly given over to storage space for farm equipment, and what the Prinettis could do with the space was limited – major alterations were out of the question. They decided to turn it into a large-scale living room. It had one entrance, originally used for tractor access, but otherwise was without light. The Prinettis added two further doors and large windows, transforming the area. Unusually, the ceiling had decorative possibilities. It was vaulted and built of mellow old bricks, so it was sanded and sealed and is now one of the architectural highlights of the ground floor.

There were few other architectural or decorative gems. The first floor was where the bedrooms for children and guests were to be

situated; the original owner had divided the area into small, relatively uninteresting spaces with very little volume, so Idarica decided that the best way to give interest and beauty to the different rooms and corridors was to use colour not only to hide structural problems but also to highlight and indeed invent new areas and give character where none existed. As a decorative painter, she used what is known as *a calce*, a water-based technique whereby the pigments are added to the wet plaster; it gives a pleasing, subtle, fresco-like effect, that gently fades with time. The colours Idarica has used – warm friendly hues – were inspired by her travels. Morocco, Turkey, and the island of Patmos, where there is a family house – all these, with their

Idarica used a water-based technique called *a calce*, whereby pigments are added to wet plaster; it gives a pleasing, subtle, fresco-like effect, that gently fades with time.

OPPOSITE The first floor glows with the rich palette that Idarica favours. In the master bedroom under the heavy eaves of the house, the deep ochre of the walls is matched by the rich red of the bed hangings and the kelim rug.

FAR LEFT The walls of upstairs corridor are gloriously decorated with rich stripes in ochre, terracotta, pink and white.

LEFT A stencilled design divides this bedroom wall into sections; designed and hand-painted by Idarica, the vertical lines of the design echo the posts of the bed, which hails from Zanzibar.

BELOW LEFT The deep ochre complements the white ceramic ware in the bathroom and makes an ideal background for pictures.

tradition of rich earth tones and natural dyestuffs, formed the basis of colour schemes seen in the house. Sometimes one colour is used to cover an entire wall; elsewhere, several colours are used in broad, thick stripes, as in the upper corridor, where the length is broken by blocks of warm, earthy tones. In one bedroom she has created a stencilled design of pale stars against a deep-red backdrop.

As with all people who understand colour and design, Idarica has used textiles in the house with regard to their intrinsic decorative worth, mixing traditional French cottons, see-through muslins and ethnic hangings, all with practised abandon. The furniture is also a mixture of the antique and the traditional, combined with the quirky and the odd piece from her travels. Indeed, the whole house is a clever, sophisticated take on a traditional, rustic home, executed in a most comfortable manner.

a colourful idyll

Montalcino is another Tuscan farmhouse that has been restored by the renowned Italian architect and decorator Piero Castellini Baldissera. Attracted by a setting that includes 'a 360-degree view across the best of the Tuscan landscape', he has succeeded in bringing that view, and the textures and colours of the landscape, into the very house itself.

Like Lavacchio (see pages 122–27), another property restored by Piero Castellini, Montalcino was formerly an abandoned farmhouse. Built in the 18th century to shelter livestock, it was in need of major restoration, although luckily it was possible to keep the original floors and ceilings, as well as most of the walls. Great care was taken to augment remnants with the best possible local materials that would enhance and even ameliorate the original.

Today Montalcino is a commanding country house, with a large vaulted-ceiling living room that runs across most of the ground floor, and with windows and doors that open on three sides to the grounds beyond and which take in many of spectacular views that make up the dramatic and attention-grabbing landscape. Also on the ground floor are a small, very pretty dining room and a cool, practical kitchen.

ABOVE The proliferation of outbuildings and barns means that Montalcino is blessed with a three-sided courtyard that offers a sheltered area on the other side of the house.

RIGHT At the kitchen end of the house, on a rough-tiled floor, is a practical all-weather hat stand, with foot and head gear appropriate for any weather, summer and winter.

FAR LEFT The views in this part of Italy are so dramatic, the buildings scattered among vines and olives, that it is not hard to see what drew Piero Castellini to the area.

Upstairs is a series of bedrooms, each decorated in an individual manner and each with its own bathroom. Although each is decorated in a different colour scheme, they share a wonderful coolness – with tiled floors, muted tones on the walls and unlined curtains on the beds and at the windows, which let the air circulate throughout the rooms. Outside, along the length of one side of the house, is a shaded dining loggia and a terrace for sitting and reading as well as eating and drinking.

The furniture at Montalcino is a combination of new and comfortable, old and beautiful, and downright quirky. It is unified with upholstery and soft furnishings that have been chosen to work together within particular soft colour palettes – another harmonious solution.

Colour is Piero's joy, and his inspiration really does come from what he sees around him in his particular world. Here, in Tuscany, it is the ochre tones of sun and the red and terracotta pinks of the earth and stones; elsewhere, on his travels, it

OPPOSITE The living room is furnished and decorated with confidence; one colour palette only has been used, based on the ochre tones of the wall; the interest comes from floor and furniture textures and the variety of designs and patterns used within a single scheme.

ABOVE AND RIGHT The small dining room acts as a cool haven in summer when the heat is too fierce, and as a comfortable retreat in other, cooler times of year.

BELOW It is their mixture of utter simplicity and refined sophistication that makes Piero Castellini Baldissera's interiors so interesting. On a plain terracotta floor, above an antique piano, is an oversized, highly decorative and decorated plaster relief, which is balanced by a collection of unrelated pieces on the lid of the piano. The composition is completed by the curved lines of an unusual horn chair.

RIGHT On an upstairs landing, an Empire daybed, covered in a contemporary striped fabric, has been placed beneath a set of 18th-century black and white prints.

FAR RIGHT The bed, with faux bamboo posts, is hung with muslin; there is no other decoration except for a chair covered in a dramatic toile de Jouy print.

Piero loves to collect the strange, the beautiful, the quirky and the individual – and mix them all together.

is the strong colours of the Mediterranean lands as well as the vibrant, immediate colours of the orient; all these he has taken, mixed together, softened and applied to the walls, creating a varied effect that effortlessly changes from room to room. He works the same sort of magic with textiles, relying sometimes on traditional classical patterns, such as 18th-century stripes or toiles, but also creating his own designs in the same palette and tradition that are designed to work in this kind of house.

Apart from his architectural and decorative skills, Piero delights in collecting the strange, the beautiful, the quirky and the individual, and mixing them together – old and new, valuable and not so valuable. This process gives him pleasure, the combination of shapes and materials sometimes grouped by a unifying colour, sometimes by a theme, and sometimes juxtaposed to provide an original or amusing contrast. Pictures are hung for effect – in one room a group of botanical prints are tightly massed; in another, 18th-century portraits in grisaille are deliberately hung against the strongest of ochre walls. It sums up the house – wherever you look, there is something to amuse or admire.

sources

ARAM
110 Drury Lane
London WC2B 5SG
020 7557 7557
www.aram.co.uk
*Classic and contemporary Italian
designs in furniture and lighting.*

B & B ITALIA
250 Brompton Road
London SW3 2AS
020 7591 8111
www.bebitalia.it
Modern Italian furniture.

A BARN FULL OF BRASS BEDS
The Farmhouse,
Ashleigh Farm, Main Road
Conisholme, Louth
Lincolnshire LN11 7LS
01507 358092
www.brassbeds.clara.net
*Restored Victorian and Edwardian
iron bedsteads.*

CERAMICA D'ARTE
020 8819 7243
www.ceramicadarte.com
*Sicilian hand-painted decorative
majolica wares sold online.*

CONTEMPORANEA
Vicolo el Babuino 8
00187 Rome
Italy
+ 39 06 323 34 65
www.contemporaneasrl@libero.it
*Distinctive contemporary
homewares.*

DIVERTIMENTI
33–34 Marylebone High Street
London W1U 4PT
020 7935 0689
and 227–229 Brompton Road
London SW3 2EP
020 7581 8065
www.divertimenti.co.uk
*A large stock of Italian
hand-painted table ceramics.*

DESIGNERS GUILD
267–277 Kings Road
London SW3 5EN
020 7351 5775
www.designersguild.com
*Italian-made range of hand-
painted ceramic tableware.*

THE FAÇADE
99 Lisson Grove
London NW1 6UP
020 7258 2017
www.thefacade.co.uk
*Decorative antiques including
chandeliers and mirrors.*

FARROW AND BALL
01202 876 141
www.farrow-ball.com
*A wide range of traditional paints
and wallpapers. Visit their website
for details of showrooms and
stockists.*

FIRED EARTH
0845 366 0400
www.firedearth.com
*Terracotta and other tiles, natural,
polished or distressed. Visit their
website for details of showrooms
and stockists.*

FRANCESCA'S LIME WASH
34 Battersea Business Centre
99–109 Lavender Hill
London SW11 5QL
020 7228 7694
www.francescaspaint.com
*Lime-wash for interior and
exterior walls plus chalky
emulsion; paints made to order.*

THE GREEN SHOP
Cheltenham Road
Bisley, Stroud
Gloucestershire GL6 7BX
01452 770629
www.greenshop.co.uk
*Natural paints and finishes;
Stuart Furby's Lime Earth Paints.
Online and catalogue sales.*

IAN MANKIN
100 Regents Park Road
London NW1 8UR
020 7722 0997
www.ianmankin.com
*Selection of muslins and
linens in all colours.*

ILARIA MIANI
Via Monserrato 35
00186 Roma
Italy
+ 39 06 683 31 60
www.ilariamiani.it
Modern Italian furniture.

THE IRON BED COMPANY
01243 380 600
www.featherandblack.com
*Wide range of new iron beds in
traditional and modern designs;
showrooms all over the country.*

PAPERS AND PAINTS
4 Park Walk
London SW10 0AD
020 7352 8626
www.papers-paints.co.uk
*Almost any colour can be mixed
from a sample.*

POLIFORM
278 Kings Road
London SW3 5AW
020 7368 7600
www.poliformuk.com
Original modern Italian furniture.

THEMES & VARIATIONS
231 Westbourne Grove
London W11 2SE
020 7727 5531
www.themesandvariations.com
*Modern Italian Furniture, including
designs by Mark Brazier-Jones.*

L'UTILE E IL DILETTEVOLE
Via Carlo Maria Maggi 6
20154 Milano
Italy
00 39 02 3453 6086
*Country antiques from Italy,
France, Britain and Sweden.*

VESSEL
114 Kensington Park Road
London W11 2PW
020 7727 8001
www.vesselgallery.com
Modern Italian art glass.

VINTAGE MODERN GLASSHOUSE
www.vmglasshouse.com
*Italian modernist art glass from the
1920s to the 1970s sold online.*

picture credits

Key: **a**=above, **b**=below, **r**=right, **l**=left, **c**=centre.
All photographs by Chris Tubbs.

Front endpapers artist Camilla d'Afflitto's home in Tuscany and studio for her paintings, architect and interior decorator Roberto Gerosa; **page 1** Marina Pignatelli's home in Val d'Orcia, Tuscany; **2** artist Camilla d'Afflitto's home in Tuscany and studio for her paintings, architect and interior decorator Roberto Gerosa; **3** a house in Maremma, Tuscany designed by Contemporanea; **4–5** Giorgio & Ilaria Miani's Podere Casellacce in Val d'Orcia; **6–7** Simon de Looze's home in Tuscany, Le Porciglia; **8–9** Marina Pignatelli's home in Val d'Orcia, Tuscany; **10–11** a house in Maremma, Tuscany designed by Contemporanea; **12l** Giorgio & Ilaria Miani's Podere Buon Riposo in Val d'Orcia; **12r & 13** Giorgio & Ilaria Miani's Podere Casellacce in Val d'Orcia; **14al** Vanni & Nicoletta Calamai's home near Siena; **14bl** Piero & Idarica Prinetti-Castelletti's 'Allevamento del Ferro' in Ottiglio, Alessandria; **14bc** a house in Tuscany planned and decorated by architect Piero Castellini Baldissera; **14–15a** Marina Pignatelli's home in Val d'Orcia, Tuscany; **14–15b** Giorgio & Ilaria Miani's Podere Casellacce in Val d'Orcia; **15a** Teresa Ginori's home near Varese; **16l** a house in Tuscany planned and decorated by architect Piero Castellini Baldissera; **16r** Giorgio & Ilaria Miani's Podere Buon Riposo in Val d'Orcia; **17a** both a house in Tuscany planned and decorated by architect Piero Castellini Baldissera; **17bl** Giorgio & Ilaria Miani's Podere Casellacce in Val d'Orcia; **17br** Giorgio & Ilaria Miani's Podere Buon Riposo in Val d'Orcia; **18a** Casa Colonica in Tuscany, interior design Isabelle de Borchgrave, architect Jean Philippe Gauvin; **18br** Toia Saibene & Giuliana Magnifico's home in Lucignano, Tuscany; **18–19a & 19a** artist Camilla d'Afflitto's home in Tuscany and studio for her paintings, architect and interior decorator Roberto Gerosa; **19br** a house in Tuscany planned and decorated by architect Piero Castellini Baldissera; **20a both** Giorgio & Ilaria Miani's Podere Casellacce in Val d'Orcia; **20br** Casa Colonica in Tuscany, interior design Isabelle de Borchgrave, architect Jean Philippe Gauvin; **21a** Mimmi O'Connell's home in Tuscany; **21b** Toia Saibene & Giuliana Magnifico's home in Lucignano, Tuscany; **22ar** Vanni & Nicoletta Calamai's home near Siena; **22al, 22br & 23** Francesco Rappini's home in Terracina; **24–25** Giorgio & Ilaria Miani's Podere Casellacce in Val d'Orcia; **26al & c** Francesco Rappini's home in Terracina; **26ac, cl, cr & br** Toia Saibene & Giuliana Magnifico's home in Lucignano, Tuscany; **26ar, 26bl & 27** Vanni & Nicoletta Calamai's home near Siena; **28–33** Toia Saibene & Giuliana Magnifico's home in Lucignano, Tuscany; **34–39** Vanni & Nicoletta Calamai's home near Siena; **46al, bc & br** Mimmi O'Connell's home in Tuscany; **46ac, ar, cl, c & bl** Giorgio & Ilaria Miani's Podere Casellacce in Val d'Orcia; **46cr** a house in Maremma, Tuscany designed by Contemporanea; **47** Giorgio & Ilaria Miani's Podere Casellacce in Val d'Orcia; **48–53** Mimmi O'Connell's home in Tuscany; **54–59** Sebastian Abbado's 'I Falchi' in Val d'Orcia; **60–65** Giorgio & Ilaria Miani's Podere Casellacce in Val d'Orcia; **66–71** a house in Maremma, Tuscany designed by Contemporanea; **72al & c** Marina Pignatelli's home in Val d'Orcia, Tuscany; **72ac** Gabriella Cantaluppi Abbado's home in Monticchiello; **72ar & cl** Casa Colonica in Tuscany, interior design Isabelle de Borchgrave, architect Jean Philippe Gauvin; **72cr & b all** artist Camilla d'Afflitto's home in Tuscany and studio for her paintings, architect and interior decorator Roberto Gerosa; **73–79** Casa Colonica in Tuscany, interior design Isabelle de Borchgrave, architect Jean Philippe Gauvin; **80–87** Marina Pignatelli's home in Val d'Orcia, Tuscany; **88–93** Gabriella Cantaluppi Abbado's home in Monticchiello; **94–99** artist Camilla d'Afflitto's home in Tuscany and studio for her paintings, architect and interior decorator Roberto Gerosa; **100–105** Teresa Ginori's home near Varese, parchment lamps and shades by architect Roberto Gerosa; **106al & bl** a house in Tuscany planned and decorated by architect Piero Castellini Baldissera; **106ac, cr & br** Giorgio & Ilaria Miani's Podere Buon Riposo in Val d'Orcia; **106ar** Simone de Looze's home in Tuscany, Le Porciglia; **106cl, c & bc** Piero & Idarica Prinetti-Castelletti's 'Allevamento del Ferro' in Ottiglio, Alessandria; **107** a house in Tuscany planned and decorated by architect Piero Castellini Baldissera; **108–15** Simone de Looze's home in Tuscany, Le Porciglia; **116–21** Giorgio & Ilaria Miani's Podere Buon Riposo in Val d'Orcia; **122–27** a house in Tuscany planned and decorated by architect Piero Castellini Baldissera; **128–33** Piero & Idarica Prinetti-Castelletti's 'Allevamento del Ferro' in Ottiglio, Alessandria, jewels by Gem Palace from We Do What We Like; **134–39** a house in Tuscany planned and decorated by architect Piero Castellini Baldissera; **back endpapers** Francesco Rappini's home in Terracina.

business credits

Camilla d'Afflitto
Via di Castel Ruggero 33
50012 Bagno a Ripoli (FI)
Italy
+ 39 055 64 99 237/222
Front endpapers, pages 2,
18–19a, 19a, 72cr, 72b all,
94–99.

Casale Rappini
Rooms available to rent
La Fiora
04010 Terracina, Latina
Italy
+ 39 077 37 72 412
frappini@libero.it
Endpapers, pages 22al, 22br, 23,
26al, 26c.

Contemporanea
Vicolo del Babuino 8
00187 Roma
Italy
+ 39 06 323 34 65
contemporaneasrl@libero.it
Pages 3, 10–11, 46cr, 66–71.

Gabriella Abbado
Designer
+ 39 333 90 30 809
Pages 72ac, 88–93.

Idarica Gazzoni
Wall decorator
Via Santa Marta 11
20123 Milano
Italy
+ 39 02 8699 7251
www.idaricagazzoni.com
Jewellery by Gem Palace
from We Do What We Like
wedoGP@tiscali.it
Pages 14bl, 106cl, 106c,
106bc, 128–33.

Ilaria Miani
Via Monserrato 35
00186 Roma
Italy
+ 39 06 683 31 60
ilariamiani@tin.it
(Podere Casellacce and Podere
Buon Riposo in Val d'Orcia are
available for rent.)
Pages 4–5, 12l, 12r, 13, 14–15b,
16r, 17bl, 17br, 20a, 24–25,
46ac, 46ar, 46cl, 46c & 46bl, 47,
60–65, 106ac, 106cr, 106br,
116–121.

Isabelle de Borchgrave
Interior Design
52 rue Gachard
B–1050 Brussels
Belgium
+ 32 (0)2 648 53 50
werner@isabelle-de-borchgrave.be

La_querciola@yahoo.fr
Pages 18a, 20br, 72ar, 72cl,
73–79.

Jean Philippe Gauvin
Architect
40 Ter avenue de Suffren
Paris 75015
France
jp.gauvin@bracqgauvin.com
Pages 18a, 20br, 72ar, 72cl,
73–79.

Mimmi O'Connell
Design Consultant
Port of Call
19 Ensor Mews
London SW7 3BT
020 7589 4836
moconnell@portofcall.co.uk
(For rental information about La
Scuola, call our London office.)
Pages 21a, 46al, 46bc 46br,
48–53.

Piero Castellini Baldissera
Architect
Via della Rocca 5
Milano
Italy
+ 39 02 4800 5384
studiocastellini@libero.it
Pages 14bc, 16l, 17a both,
19br, 106al, 106bl, 107,
122–27, 134–39.

Sebastian Abbado
Project developer–architectural
design, urban reconstruction and
landscaping
+ 44 (0)7899 790459
Also involved in this project:
Luigi Vivarelli (bed metal worker)
+ 39 578 758 728
(mobile + 39 347 391 9911)
Benedetta Brunotti
+ 39 347 697 87 68
Lorenzo Capaccio
+ 39 349 779 79 28
Pages 54–59.

Simone de Looze
Interiors
+ 39 335 572 06 85
akadelooze@inwind.it
Also involved in this project:
Anthony Collett
Collett–Zarzycki
Fernhead Studios
2b Fernhead Road
London W9 3ET
020 8969 6967
www.collett-zarzycki.com
Pages 6–7, 106ar, 108–115.

Teresa Ginori
teresa.ginori@aliceposta.it
Pages 15a, 100–105.

index

Page numbers in *italics* denote illustrations.

acknowledgments

The publishers would like to thank the following people for their help with locations: Enrica Stabile, Teresa Ginori, Lorenza Bianda Pasquinelli, Julia Brown, Cristina Le Grazie and Lisa Gabriel. Thank you also to all the owners who allowed us to photograph their beautiful homes and made us feel so welcome.

Chris Tubbs would like to thank all the people whose amazing houses were a pleasure to photograph. Their hospitality and generosity was touching. He would also like to thank Ryland Peters & Small for making the experience possible, particularly Gabriella, without whom it would not have been so enjoyable. And, finally, thanks to Rachel Barber for making me so happy. Bonjour, Coco!